A REFUTATION OF MORAL RELATIVISM:
INTERVIEWS WITH AN ABSOLUTIST

A REFUTATION OF MORAL RELATIVISM

INTERVIEWS WITH AN ABSOLUTIST

BY
PETER KREEFT

IGNATIUS PRESS   SAN FRANCISCO

Cover design by Roxanne Mei Lum

© 1999 Ignatius Press, San Francisco
All rights reserved
ISBN 0–89870–731–5
Library of Congress catalogue number 98–75209
Printed in the United States of America ∞

Dedicated to

Thomas Aquinas,
Moses Maimonides,
and Al-Ghazali

Contents

Technical Note

All the characters, places, and events in this book are real. However, the author took the liberty of changing the names of the characters and the location of the events. The interviews actually took place not in my house on Martha's Vineyard but in my house in Boston, which is a real place (except to New Yorkers) and in my mind, which is a real mind (except to New Age thinkers). 'Isa Ben Adam and Libby Rawls really live there, but they have no Social Security numbers, and though I call them by their separate names, others call them both by the name Peter Kreeft.

Introduction

The Title

I hope my subtitle will not suggest parallels to Anne Rice's wicked best-seller *Interview with a Vampire*. But I fear it will, since the image of a moral absolutist that has been branded into our minds by our media is barely distinguishable from that of a vampire. It is something darkly dogmatic and heavybootedly hypocritical—a kind of Fundamentalist Fascist.

Let it be so, then. If that is what an absolutist is, then interviewing one should be as fascinating as interviewing a vampire. Come, then, to the freak show. Buy this book, your admission ticket to peer into the weedy deeps of the psyche of the monster: Swamp Thing, Grendel, Nessie. See the last dinosaur before the species becomes as dead as the dodo.

The Characters

I do not know quite how to classify this book: interview, conversation, or debate? It is a series of dialogues between two of the most fascinating and delightful friends I have ever had the great good fortune to meet.

'Isa Ben Adam, the interviewee, is a forty-one-year-old Palestinian Arab who is a Professor of Philosophy at the American University in Beirut, Lebanon. However, I can't call him "Professor", as his interviewer does; I've always called him "'Isa". I met him in 1978, when he was my student at Boston College. He is probably the most brilliant student I have ever taught, and certainly the most interesting. I see him as an integrated multiple personality made up of equal parts of Doctor Samuel Johnson, Malcolm Muggeridge, Alexandr Solzhenitsyn, G. K. Chesterton, Hilaire Belloc, Judge Robert Bork, and Alasdair MacIntyre.

I want to call 'Isa's mind a knife, but a knife can't be both blunt and sharp at the same time, as he is. *Formidable* is the word that pushes forward out of the mass of adjectives that compete to describe him, but pronounced with properly Frankish gravity and awe: "foer-mee-*dah*-bl"! He does not suffer fools gladly, and Americans tend to find some of his mannerisms impolite and insensitive. However, though gruff or even cantankerous, he is far from humorless. (He was at Oxford for a time, and I think his soul is still there.) Many people, including his interviewer, find him arrogant—and if he had not suffered much when he was younger, he would probably be insufferable; but I find him humble—humble enough to forget about his appearance or "persona" and attack the issue or the argument like a warrior. If people were elements, 'Isa would be fire. (Perhaps that is why he is so in love with water and the sea.)

The interviewer, Liberty ("Libby") Rawls, is a journalist who has been called "a classy, sassy Black feminist". She has *lived* as much as 'Isa has *thought*, having been a wife, a psychological social worker, a surfing instructor, an actress, an alcoholic, and a private investigator, as well as a journalist. She has known 'Isa since 1978, when they and seven others shared a rooming house in Nahant, Massachusetts. Both Libby and 'Isa credit its owner, Maria Kirk, with saving their lives. But that's another story.

Libby and 'Isa had many conversations at that house—more accurately, many heated arguments ending with slammed doors more often than with syllogisms. Both are now supposed to be in their "professional mode", but their personal history continually peeks through —which is exactly what I foresaw and calculated would add a bit of personal drama to the argumentative drama. So I persuaded them to record these interviews by the bribe of a week of great swimming, fishing, sailing, and surfing at the prettiest little four-room Victorian gingerbread cottage ("The Purple Angel") on the prettiest island in the world (Martha's Vineyard).

The interviews were tape recorded there during the summer of 1998 (a twenty-year-later anniversary party) and transcribed into this book with nothing added or omitted. They are more like an argument between friends than the typical journalist's interview of a celebrity, in which the journalist is either a lapdog or a vulture. Libby is no match for 'Isa in philosophical debate, but neither is she a mere "journalist". Her mind is sharp and her questions pointed and honest. They are the questions most people have about moral absolutism, whether they read Plato's *Republic* or the *National Enquirer*.

The Topic

The question discussed is: *Are there moral absolutes?* Three groups of people will find these interviews of great interest:

1. Anyone perceptive enough to realize that the issue may be the single most crucial issue of our time, the most practical issue, since it makes the greatest difference to our lives. Nothing more radically distinguishes our culture (the modern West) from all others in human history, including the premodern West as well as contemporary non-Western cultures, whether Islamic, communist, or "primitive". Most of our culture's intellectual leaders find the moral absolutisms of all these other cultures not only false but also dangerous, while these other cultures, in turn, find our relativism and scepticism of their moral certainties not only false but also dangerous—like a giant without a conscience. That is why many pious (and impious) Muslims call America "the great Satan".

2. Anyone who wonders what respectable logical arguments (as distinct from prejudices, fears, or provincialisms) could possibly be given by an absolutist to defend his outdated philosophy. 'Isa Ben Adam may be right or he may be wrong, but he is certainly very clear and very intelligent.

3. Anyone interested in the psychological dimension of the issue, for the two positions are here incarnated in two characters who seem typical of the two different philosophies. The interviewer is "liberal", sceptical, tolerant, and openminded. (An absolutist would probably call her philosophy "wishy-washy".) The interviewee is very "conservative", convinced, and uncompromising. (A relativist would probably call him "dogmatic" and "intolerant".) Beneath the mutual insults there is much more friendship and respect between these two individuals than there usually is between the two groups they represent, and they got along much better in "real life" (in the house, on the beach, in the boat) than appeared in these "interviews".

Interview 1

The Importance of Moral Relativism:
Will It Really "Damn Our Souls
and End Our Species?"

Libby: Is the tape running?

Kreeft: I can't guarantee that. I probably pushed the wrong button. Any machine more complicated than a pen spooks me out.

Libby: Here, let me see. It's OK. My goodness, Dr. Kreeft, don't you use a computer?

Kreeft: I do, but a clever little demon lives inside it. It's a *Lurker*, and it lurks patiently till it sees me hit the wrong button, and then it pounces on my words and gobbles them up and takes them away to hell.

Libby: Have you considered an exorcist? Surely among all those Jesuits at Boston College . . . ?

'Isa: The tape's running. Shouldn't we begin the serious stuff? The interview?

Kreeft: Demons *are* serious stuff, for some of us.

Libby: And computers, for others.

'Isa: And for still others, the topic of our interview: Are there moral absolutes?

Libby: Touché, Professor. So can we begin?

'Isa: Please.

Libby: Our first interview is supposed to be about the issue itself—what moral absolutism means and why you think it's so important to think about it. Then we'll bite into the substance of it, the actual arguments, the evidence pro and con. We sort of whet the appetite for the steak to come by having a cocktail first.

'Isa: Not just to whet the appetite, but to save time . . .

Libby: What do you mean?

'Isa: I was about to explain.

Libby: Sorry.

'Isa: Time is life. Our "life time". Stupid to waste it on secondary things. William James, one of your most sensible philosophers, thought that most of the questions philosophers fool around with weren't worth the time because they *made no difference.* That's his criterion: Does it make a difference to our experience whether a given idea is believed to be true or false? If not, it can't be true in any meaningful sense, if it makes no real difference. Waste no time on it, then; it's pettifoggery or dilettantism.

Libby: The pragmatic criterion of truth. Yes, I like that. Truth really means *relevance.*

'Isa: No it doesn't. James was confused there, and so are you. Truth means truth, and relevance means relevance. But only some truths are relevant, and those are the only ones worth spending time on. That's where James was right. And so are you. So let's first be sure that this truth *is* relevant, or important.

Libby: That's what this first interview is all about, I think: Why should we think about this abstract question? Why is it so important for all of us, for our lives? So may I ask you that question now, Professor, in my own way?—the way I think most people today who *aren't* professors are asking it?

'Isa: Don't ask permission; just do it.

Libby: Yes, indeed. Well, then, I'd like to begin by looking at moral absolutism as a sociological option, rather than a philosophical one. You're certainly very much aware of the violence going on in Islamic countries like Iran and Iraq and interreligious warfare in Lebanon and Syria and Palestine. I think most Americans and Europeans view moral absolutism with alarm because they see a connection there. No, just let me finish my question, please, OK? Let me explain why most

Americans are afraid of moral absolutism, and then you can address their fears, OK? I think most Americans see two very different kinds of countries in the world: free countries—pluralistic democracies—and monolithic countries that enforce their version of moral absolutism, some official orthodoxy—whether Islamic or communist or Catholic or whatever—and they simply do not tolerate dissent, or pluralism, or diversity. Now I'm not saying there aren't serious problems in free and democratic countries—everyone knows that—crime and poverty and racism and private violence—and a lot of individuals just fall through the cracks. But most Americans see much bigger problems in absolutist societies. That's why they opt for a pluralist, free society despite all the problems that so much freedom brings with it. And they address those problems not by abolishing the freedom and pluralism and tolerance that may allow some of these problems to arise, but by education, and law and by financing social programs to combat the poverty and violence and drugs and unwanted pregnancies and other social problems. We try to patch the leaks on the ship instead of jumping ship, instead of jumping to an absolutist ship instead—*any* absolutism, whether Christian or Jewish or Islamic or communist or whatever. Do you disagree with this view, Professor? I know you do. How do you as a moral absolutist address these fears? You see, Americans don't look at the issue of absolutism by abstract logic and philosophical arguments but by sociological evidence that's concrete, that they can see right in front of them in society. So what do you as a philosopher say about that evidence?

'**Isa:** So you *do* want me to start arguing instead of just explaining the importance of the issue.

Libby: No, just explain how you see the social importance of the issue first.

'**Isa:** Why first? It *isn't* first; it's second.

Libby: Second to what? To philosophy?

'**Isa:** Second to people, to individuals. Societies are made by people, and made *of* people, and made *for* people—or have you forgotten President Lincoln's formula "government of the people, by the people, and for the people"?

Libby: Oh, that's a great formula, and I love it too. No, I didn't mean *government* first, or *politics* first. I meant let's look at *society* first, culture first, then the individual who's conditioned by the culture. The people first, then the person.

'Isa: But suppose I don't believe the group *should* be first, before the individual?

Libby: I only asked you to address the social *question* first. I didn't ask you to believe that society really does come first, or really should come first. Just a question, an approach—the one most Americans take, I think. So if you want to meet them where they are coming from—well, meet them there.

'Isa: All right, let's see—where to start? Let's start in . . . Auschwitz. That's the fruit of moral relativism. Is that relevant enough for you?

Libby: You haven't proved the connection, Professor; you've just assigned the blame, dogmatically—blamed Auschwitz on your favorite whipping boy, moral relativism. Why not blame it on moral absolutism?

'Isa: You want concrete evidence? I'll let Mussolini answer that question, OK? Here, let me find the quotation—Mussolini was something of a philosopher, you know—hmm . . . ah, here it is. Listen to what he wrote: "Everything I have said and done in these last years is relativism by intuition. . . . If relativism signifies contempt for fixed categories and men who claim to be the bearers of an objective, immortal truth . . . then there is nothing more relativistic than fascistic attitudes and activity. . . . From the fact that all ideologies are of equal value, that all ideologies are mere fictions, the modern relativist infers that everybody has the right to create for himself his own ideology and to attempt to enforce it with all the energy of which he is capable." That's from Mussolini's *Diuturna*, pages 374–77.

Libby: But Professor, America isn't fascist, America isn't Auschwitz. Are you saying it is?

'Isa: No, but I'm saying it's buying into the philosophy that led to Auschwitz in Germany.

Libby: How? Do you see Auschwitz happening here?

'Isa: No, that was the hard version of relativism. Here, it's leading to *Brave New World*—the soft version of relativism.

Libby: I'm sorry, Professor, but I've got to say I'm deeply disappointed so far. I thought this interview was going to be something like a debate, or at least like a university lecture, where you'd have to *prove* things and *explain* things. It sounds more like demagoguery to me so far—name calling instead of logical arguments and demonstrations and data. I thought you were going to be scientific and logical . . .

'Isa: I *will* be. Here's a logical argument for you, then—one based on data, massive historical data. Here is my data: the modern West is the first society in history whose mind molders are moral relativists. No other society in history has ever survived without rejecting moral relativism and believing in moral absolutes. There has never been a society of relativists, any more than a society of solipsists. Therefore, this society will either disprove one of the most universally established laws of history, or repent of its relativism and survive, or persist in its relativism and perish.

Libby: And by "this society" you mean . . . ?

'Isa: I mean the modern West: democratic, pluralistic, secular, scientific, technological, industrial, post-Enlightenment civilization. Geographically, that's Europe and its former colonies. Theologically, that's apostate Christendom.

Libby: So you see it as a religious issue rather than a social issue?

'Isa: Not "rather than". But of course it's a religious issue.

Libby: Because it has religious causes, faith assumptions . . .

'Isa: Because it has religious *effects*, religious consequences. To quote C. S. Lewis in "The Poison of Subjectivism", relativism "will certainly damn our souls and end our species". (By the way, please remember that Oxford philosophers are not given to exaggeration.)

Libby: And you agree with that?

'Isa: Yes.

Libby: Why did Lewis think it will "damn our souls"?

'Isa: Because Lewis was a Christian, so he could not disagree with the teaching of Jesus and of all the prophets in Jesus' Jewish tradition —and, later, Islamic tradition too . . .

Libby: What teaching?

'Isa: The teaching that in order to be saved, to go to heaven, you need to repent. But you can't repent if you don't believe in sin to repent of, and you can't believe in sin if you don't believe in a real moral law, because sin means disobeying *that*. Moral relativism eliminates that law, thus sin, thus repentance, thus salvation.

Libby: Wow! So a pop psychologist can't be saved, then?

'Isa: Not without conversion.

Libby: Wow! Can I tell my psychologist friends that on the authority of Professor 'Isa Ben Adam?

'Isa: No, on the authority of my namesake. *Jesus* said that, didn't he? "I did not come to call the self-righteous, but to call sinners, to repentance."

Libby: And you also agree that moral relativism will "end our species"?

'Isa: Yes—though that's a triviality compared with damning our souls for eternity.

Libby: A triviality! I'll let that go for now. Tell me, why the whole species, and not just the one civilization that believes it, namely, white Western man?

'Isa: As distinct from Black Eastern woman?

Libby: If you must put it that way.

'Isa: Because there *is* no society called Black Eastern woman.
    [At this point the tape has Libby muttering something inarticulate.]

Libby: Let me just ask you again: Why our whole species?

'Isa: Because your whole species is becoming Westernized . . .

Libby: "*Your*" species? You speak as an outsider, Professor?

'Isa: Is this supposed to be an interview or a debate?

Libby: All right, an interview. So you see a kind of Western cultural imperialism going on throughout the world?

'Isa: Everyone knows that. From Zambia to China you now hear American music . . .

Libby: Rock, you mean.

'Isa: Yes.

Libby: And rap.

'Isa: I was talking about *music.*

Libby: Ha! So do you believe the world will end if everyone buys Calvin Klein jeans?

'Isa: No, I believe the world will end if everyone buys Calvin Klein sex.

Libby: So you see American culture as a kind of cancer that's metastasizing throughout the globe?

'Isa: Yes. I don't shrink back from offensive metaphors.

Libby: I can see that.

'Isa: In fact, I'd call America Dracula and all other cultures its victims. They're getting paler and paler. Soon all the blood will be gone.

Libby: Are you Doctor Van Helsing, then? And what is the wooden stake you would put through Dracula's heart?

'Isa: This interview! Or, rather, these arguments. This refutation of relativism. If it's ever published, that will make thousands of little wooden stakes for thousands of little Doctor Van Helsings, who read it. Anyone can do it. Anyone can kill Dracula. It's the power of the truth that will do it, not the power of the person. The power of the light. Just open the shade and let the light of the sun in, and Dracula will wither and scream and die.

Libby: I see. Professor, don't you think your doomsday scenario runs afoul of facts? Look at America. This "Dracula", as you call it, is one of the most religious countries in the world. Half the people go to church, and 95% believe in God. America's got more religion than almost any other country.

'Isa: Yes, and it's also got more guns, more suicides, more abortions, more divorces, more drugs, more pornography, more fatherless children than almost any other country.

Libby: How can that be? Doesn't that refute religion's claims? Isn't religion supposed to be the *cure* for all these social diseases?

'Isa: Not if the religion is as relativistic as the society. Not if the doctor is as sick as the patient. A God made in the world's image can't save the world. You see, American religion wants to make you feel good and be comfortable, not to shock you or scandalize you.

Libby: And you prefer shocks and scandals?

'Isa: It's not a matter of my preferences. It's the nature of things, it's built in. Look, I'm just being realistic and logical. If we're sinking in quicksand, we can't pull ourselves out by our own bootstraps. Man-made religion can't raise man one inch. If *we* make the religion, we spread our infection in it; so in the very process of trying to operate on our infection, we infect ourselves more. It's like a needle we invent to cure our disease, but it's *our* needle, so it's got our disease germs on it. So in the very act of giving ourselves an injection of man-made religion, we inject ourselves more with the disease.

Libby: So do you think religions are man-made, or not?

'Isa: Many are. And look at the results.

Libby: What results?

'Isa: In a word, Babel.

Libby: The Tower of Babel story?

'Isa: Yes. Babel, Babylon, Baal, paganism, modern paganism, gods made in our own image. It all comes to the same thing, the same result, in the end.

Libby: What result is that?

'Isa: Read Genesis 10. The Tower of Babel story. The tower has to fall. And *then* comes Abraham.

Libby: Abraham?

'Isa: The one God picked out. First, man tries to build up to God, build a civilization on human foundations—that's the Tower of Babel.

It was supposed to reach to heaven. It collapses, because its human foundation is too weak for that long a journey. Then God comes down to Abraham with the real religion. That's like an upside-down Tower of Babel. That's the beginning of what the New Testament calls the New Jerusalem, the real Tower that comes down from God out of heaven. It works because its foundation is in heaven. God can build a bridge, or a tower, down to earth; but earth can't build one to heaven.

Libby: I don't really see the point of your images. What does this have to do with moral relativism?

'Isa: Moral relativism denies an absolute law for man. It says good and evil are man-made. Its morality and its religion *are* the Tower of Babel. How can you not see it?

Libby: You're identifying morality and religion, then? An honest atheist can't be good?

'Isa: No, I'm not saying that at all. An honest atheist who pursues truth and goodness will find it. And a theist who doesn't, won't.

Libby: "Seek and you shall find", eh?

'Isa: Yes. The seeker has already taken the first step. "Seeking" means loving. That's the heart, or the will, that does the loving. His heart is already converted: he's in love with truth and goodness. Then comes the second step: finding. That's the conversion of the head. That will come if the first step is there.

Libby: I see.

'Isa: But a religious believer who knows the true and the good in his head but who doesn't love it in his heart and his life—he won't submit to it, he wants to make it relative to his desires, relative to what his heart really loves and wants and seeks—he'll lose even the truth and goodness he already has by making it relative to himself, *his* heart, *his* will, *his* desires, *his* demands. He won't *submit* his heart to truth. That's the essence of all true religion: submission of the heart to truth, to God, to what God is: truth and moral goodness. That's why I say that the honest and moral atheist is a religious man and the relativistic churchgoer is not. The atheist really wants to submit to the truth; he just doesn't know what the truth is. The relativistic churchgoer has had the truth given to him, and he doesn't like it, he doesn't want to submit to it, he won't convert his heart and life to it. So he chooses to change it instead of letting it change him. He wants to sing "I Did It My Way". You see the difference? That's why Jesus said seekers find, and that's why Paul told the Greek philosophers in Athens that they were already worshipping the true God, whom Paul would now reveal to them. Even though these pagans had a lot of idols, false gods, they were *seeking* for the true God. So Paul said, "The God you are worshipping, I now declare to you." They had already submitted their hearts; now their minds followed. The modern relativistic churchgoer is exactly the opposite, you see. Their minds know the truth, but their hearts don't love it, don't submit to it, so they give it up, they exchange it for a lie: the comfortable relativistic lie that they don't have to submit. And so they cease even to *know* the truth. It's the "first things" principle: put first things first, and second things will follow; refuse to put the first thing first, and you'll lose the second things too.

Libby: And the "first thing" is the love of truth?

'Isa: Yes.

Libby: And the "second thing" is the knowledge of it?

'Isa: Yes.

Libby: And the connection with *morality* is . . . ?

'Isa: Don't you see it? The love of *true* morality, objectively true morality, moral truth—that's what relativism refuses. Moral relativism denies the very first thing, the foundation for all morality. That's why it's so devastating. It's not just an inaccurate theory about morality, a *mistake*. It's a *refusal*, the refusal to submit.

Libby: To your particular absolutist morality.

'Isa: No, no, no! To *truth*.

Libby: To *your* truth.

'Isa: "*Your*" truth? That's a self-contradiction. It's oxymoronic. It's also moronic.

Libby: Thanks for the compliment.

'Isa: Just look at the *issue*, won't you?

Libby: I thought the issue was moral relativism versus moral absolutism.

'Isa: It is, but the issue is not just acceptance or rejection of moral absolutism as a *theory about* morality, a *philosophy*. It's much more than that. That's why salvation depends on it, on what we might call the absolutism of truth, of submitting to truth. *That's* the fundamental requirement for salvation. And for honesty. Let me try to explain. If I believed that the philosophical theory called moral absolutism were objectively false, not objectively true, but I embraced it anyway, because I felt like it, I'd be refusing to submit to truth. Or if I didn't *care* whether it was true or false, but I embraced it anyway, for some other reason—any other reason besides truth—I'd be refusing to submit to truth.

Libby: I see. Then if I embrace moral relativism because I think it's true, I *am* submitting to truth.

'Isa: Yes!

Libby: So I'm really a moral absolutist, then.

'Isa: Yes, in principle. You're submitting to the first moral law, "Seek the Truth". So eventually you'll find the rest of it, if you really want to.

Libby: Oh. I'm . . . frankly, I'm surprised at this personal turn the dialogue has taken. Do you really believe that, 'Isa?

'Isa: Certainly.

Libby: About me, I mean?

'Isa: Yes, Libby, I really do.

Libby: Oh. Well. . . . Frankly, I'm at a loss how to continue. I'd like to digest that last point you made, about the heart, if you don't mind. I guess that's being a bit unprofessional for an interviewer, but . . .

'Isa: It's OK, Libby. It's a good place to stop. We all talk too much and think too little. Let's both stop talking and think about this for a while.

Libby: Great. A walk on the beach is what I need right now.

Kreeft: The sea will teach you without words.

'Isa: Even without thoughts.

Libby: I've noticed that. How does it do that, I wonder?

Kreeft: Seepage.

Libby: Seepage?

Kreeft: The water seeps under your mind's foundations.

'Isa: And into your heart.

Interview 2

What *Is* Moral Relativism?

Kreeft: I think this interview will be the dullest one; that's why we should probably keep it short.

'Isa: I don't agree. Every Socratic dialogue was about defining a term, remember? But *they* certainly weren't dull. Why should ours have to be dull?

Libby: I hope you're right. OK, let's go. The tape's running. Let's define our terms, starting with *moral absolutism* and *moral relativism*, and let's also define our goal in these interviews.

'Isa: Yes, let's. I take it we are to limit the scope to a single point that we might hope really to prove one way or the other, so that we don't dance around a hundred different points and really prove none of them.

Libby: Aha! So you've already tipped your hand. You've already pre-set the goal of these interviews as *proving* moral absolutism.

'Isa: Certainly.

Libby: Certainly, huh? Not just giving good reasons for it or a good case for it?

'Isa: No, to prove it and to *refute* relativism.

Libby: Refute it?

'Isa: To strip it naked, to unmask it, to humiliate it, to give it the *whuppin'* it deserves.

Libby: You were in Texas last week, weren't you?

'Isa: Yes . . .

Libby: Your goals are not modest.

'**Isa:** But we won't prove anything yet tonight. Tonight we merely define our terms.

Libby: Then tonight I guess I'm not supposed to do much—just be a good little student and ask a few obvious questions and not make any trouble. And you're going to act more like a professor.

'**Isa:** I hope I can give a fair imitation.

Libby: So can you define *relativism* for us, Professor?

'**Isa:** Yes. Relativism is the philosophy that denies absolutes. *Any* absolutes. *Everyone* believes there are many relativities, that *some* things are relative; but relativism claims that *all* things are relative.

Libby: That seems very clear.

'**Isa:** Except that there are different kinds of relativism. I can think of at least four important kinds that we have to distinguish: metaphysical relativism, epistemological relativism, moral relativism, and religious relativism. You can claim there are no absolutes anywhere in reality —that's metaphysical relativism. Or anywhere in human knowledge —that's epistemological relativism. Or anywhere in morality—that's moral relativism. Or anywhere in religion—that's religious relativism.

Libby: So is religious relativism the same as atheism?

'**Isa:** No. *Metaphysical* relativism is the same as atheism (assuming "God" means the "Absolute Being"). Metaphysics is about being. Religion is about relationships with the Absolute Being. So religious relativism says there's no absolute religion, no absolutely best or truest religious relationship with God. Atheism says there's no God, no Absolute Being, no absolute anywhere in reality.

Libby: What's epistemological relativism?

'**Isa:** It says, "Perhaps there is a metaphysical absolute, an Absolute Being, somewhere; but it can't be *known*. There's no absolute in human *knowledge*."

Libby: So epistemological relativism means scepticism.

'**Isa:** Scepticism about the Absolute, at least, or agnosticism. Or it could be total scepticism, scepticism about all reality.

Libby: And now where does moral relativism fit in?

'Isa: Well, metaphysical relativism says, "No absolute in reality", and epistemological relativism says, "Perhaps in reality but not in knowledge", and then moral relativism says, "Perhaps there are absolutes in *nonmoral* knowledge, like 'two plus two make four', but not in *moral* knowledge: we know no moral absolutes." And then, finally, religious relativism says, "Perhaps in moral knowledge but not in religious knowledge. Perhaps love, or the Golden Rule, or justice, can be known to be absolute, but no religion can."

Libby: And why do we need to define these other three relativisms to talk about moral relativism?

'Isa: So we can distinguish it from them and confine ourselves to it.

Libby: All right. So now let's focus more exactly on what you mean by moral relativism and moral absolutism.

'Isa: We need to define the two words *moral* and *absolutism*. Let's take *moral* first. How do we use that word? It's used to refer to a quality of people and their deeds, interior and exterior, that we express by the words *good* and *bad*, or *good* and *evil*. But not all good is *moral* good: a good car, for instance. So more specifically, moral good and bad means *right and wrong*. Even there, we have to be more specific, since something can be "right" without being *morally* right: the right answer to a puzzle, for instance. So let's say morality is about what we *ought* to do and ought not to do. Another word for *ought* is an *imperative,* or an *obligation.* I think everyone understands what *moral* means, from ordinary language usage, so I'd rather not go any deeper into questions philosophers have about defining that term now. I'd like to stick to ordinary language and talk to ordinary people.

Libby: Thank you, Professor Extraordinaire. And now what about defining absolutism and relativism?

'Isa: As I said, relativism says there are no absolutes. Absolutely no absolutes. Absolutism says there are *some* absolutes. At least *one* absolute. Absolutism is relatively absolutistic, and relativism is absolutely relativistic.

Libby: Ah, we're going to refute relativism by a brilliant word-juggling trick, I see.

'Isa: No, we're not. We're going to give ordinary language meanings, that's all.

Libby: Then what does *relative* mean, and what does *absolute* mean?

'Isa: *Relative* is always "relative *to* something else", contingent upon something else, conditional upon something else. *Absolute* means "*not* relative", not contingent but necessary, not conditioned but unconditioned. No ifs, ands, or buts.

Libby: Could you give examples?

'Isa: Certainly. "Don't steal if it hurts anybody" is a relative moral imperative. "Don't steal, period" is an absolute one.

Libby: What Kant called a "Categorical Imperative".

'Isa: Yes. But "Be good to others if and when you want them to be good to you" is not a moral absolute. "Be good to others always" is.

Libby: So absolutes are unchangeable.

'Isa: Yes, and universal, and objective. Those are the three characteristics that distinguish an absolute. It is not relative to *time*, so it doesn't change. And it's not relative to *place* or nation or class or culture or race or gender or any group—it's universal. Third, it's not relative to *opinion* or thought or belief or desire or feeling or any subjective consciousness. It's objectively real, objectively true, whether I or you or anyone else knows it, or believes it, or likes it, or cares about it, or obeys it.

Libby: So personal opinions and beliefs and feelings and motivations and intentions—they don't change morality?

'Isa: No . . .

Libby: So intentions aren't important, only the rules?

'Isa: No, that's not right. Some moral rules are *about* intentions. Others are about external deeds. For instance, "don't be greedy" is about intentions, and "don't steal" is about deeds. But both are absolute. Greed and theft are both wrong—always wrong, for everyone. No exceptions.

Libby: So a good intention doesn't make a deed good?

'Isa: It doesn't make a *bad* deed good.

Libby: So love isn't enough? A sincere, loving intention isn't enough? Is that what you're saying?

'Isa: That's what I'm saying. If I kill you because I'm sincerely trying to help the poor by killing the rich, that's still a bad deed.

Libby: So only deeds count, not intentions?

'Isa: No, both count. You need both good deeds and good intentions. Neither one can substitute for the other. A good deed doesn't change a bad intention into a good one, so a good intention doesn't change a bad deed into a good one either.

Libby: And what about situations? Changing situations don't change morality either, according to your absolutism?

'Isa: No, they change how you should apply the rules, but they don't change the rules.

Libby: So it's just as wrong for Jean Valjean in *Les Misérables* to steal a loaf of bread to feed his starving family as it is for Blackbeard the Pirate to steal the King's gold to make himself rich? Is that what you're saying?

'Isa: No, I say Jean Valjean did not steal at all. He had a right to that food. Blackbeard had no right to the gold.

Libby: I see. So the situation doesn't ever change stealing from wrong to right, but it sometimes changes *taking* from stealing to not stealing.

'Isa: Very well put, Libby.

Libby: I'm not your student, Professor. I'm your interviewer.

'Isa: Oh. Sorry.

Libby: Let's be sure I understand this. You're a moral absolutist, but you'd say it was morally right for a Dutch family who were hiding Jews from the Nazis to lie to the Nazis when they came to search the house, right? I mean you'd say that *wasn't* lying at all, because the Nazis had no right to know. Is that right?

'Isa: Yes. The Nazis had no right to know that truth, and the Jews had a right to conceal it, and the Dutch had a right to deceive the Nazis about it—an obligation, even. So it wasn't wrong. *Lying* is always wrong, and that wasn't wrong, so that wasn't a lie, just as Jean Valjean taking the bread wasn't a theft. So the absolutes remain: never lie, never steal.

Libby: So what would the *relativist* say about those two situations? She'd say that Jean's taking *was* a theft, but sometimes theft is good, and that the Dutch family lied, but sometimes lying is good—so isn't the difference only in words?—a matter of whether you paste the label "lie" on the act or not? We all agree what acts are moral, don't we?

'Isa: Of course not. If we did, we wouldn't be arguing about things like abortion and homosexuality and euthanasia and cloning.

Libby: Oh. But those things are specific. Don't you think the most *general* principles, or general beliefs about morality, are the same for both the moral relativist and the moral absolutist? I'm not sure just how to word this. Doesn't everyone say we should take morality seriously? Have you ever heard anyone say "to hell with morality"? Or "it's bad to be good"?

'Isa: No, but I've certainly heard "it's good to be bad".

Libby: So relativism says it's good to be bad?

'Isa: No, relativism says it's only relatively good to be good.

Libby: You're confusing me with your clever words. As my mother used to say, you're dropping words so fast, I have to be careful where I step.

'Isa: Is this an interview or a debate? Am I allowed to return her insults?

Kreeft: No, and she's not supposed to give them either. Can you both try to be less anal and more analytical?

'Isa: I like that! We need to analyze exactly what we're talking about today and what we want to talk about tomorrow. We're *defining* moral relativism today and *refuting* it tomorrow and the next day.

Libby: Thank you, Professor. And will you define and refute the other relativisms too? Metaphysical relativism and epistemological relativism?

'Isa: No. One argument at a time is enough. But we may look at them briefly, toward the end, because they're connected with moral relativism. They're a common cause of moral relativism.

Libby: And what about other relativisms? Einstein's theory of relativity, for instance?

'Isa: No, I'm not a physicist, and I don't claim to be able to prove or disprove that. But that's not a cause of moral relativism.

Libby: A lot of people think it is.

'Isa: That's silly. Because matter curves space, and light has finite speed, therefore it's OK to kill your grandmother? There's no connection.

Libby: What about this connection, Professor? According to the theory of physical relativity, we can't measure any motion absolutely and objectively and accurately, because we're moving too. So we can't measure what's right and wrong for any other moving minds because ours is moving too. We can't be wholly objective.

'Isa: But we can! Even in physics we can know and measure our own motions, and compensate for them, and measure others' motions objectively and accurately. Ask any air traffic controller.

Libby: But only relative to some arbitrary standard, like the ground. And we have to ignore the fact that that's moving too, relative to something else, like the sun. Nothing stands still. There's no unchanging absolute.

'Isa: Not in matter. You're right about physics, I think. But physics isn't morality.

Libby: "Physics isn't morality"—it's as simple as that?

'Isa: Yes it is. If you say morality should be relative just because physics is, why not say morality should be mathematical just as physics is? Why not demand a quantum morality? It's just stupid.

Libby: Thank you, Professor.

'Isa: I didn't say *you* were stupid, Libby. I said your idea was stupid.

Libby: Ideas don't have brains or feelings, Professor. People do.

'Isa: You know, this is beginning to sound like 1978.

Libby: Should we just give it up, do you think?

'Isa: Certainly not.

Libby: Why? If we can't do an objective interview, let's not try.

'Isa: If *you* can't do it, you mean. You're the interviewer.

Libby: And you're the idiot—just as insufferable now as you were twenty years ago.

'Isa: So why don't you just stomp out of the room and slam the door? That's how you used to refute all my arguments then.

Libby: Would it be so awful if we gave up? What would that be?

'Isa: Failure.

Libby: And what would you have us do?

'Isa: Succeed.

Libby: How?

'Isa: The way my papa taught me: "If at first you don't succeed, try, try again."

Libby: OK, let's try again tomorrow. But it better come out better than today.

'Isa: It'll be more interesting, anyway. Tomorrow we argue.

Libby: Oh, yeah, sure. Tonight all we did was kissy-face.

Interview 3

The History of Relativism

Libby: Professor, I think today's topic ought to be a good one to get us back on track after our little regression yesterday evening. Past history is something we're not responsible for—we two individuals, I mean—so it should be easier for us to discuss it objectively. And today we're scheduled to explore the history of moral absolutism and moral relativism.

'Isa: No, just moral relativism. Absolutism has no history.

Libby: What ever do you mean?

'Isa: It's perennial; it's natural; it's from the beginning. In fact, it's eternal. It begins in heaven. But relativism begins on earth, in time.

Libby: Well, whether absolutism began in heaven or not, our research into the history of earth won't extend *that* far, so let's just talk about history today, all right?

'Isa: All right.

Libby: You say absolutism came first in history, not relativism. How do you know that?

'Isa: Because all cultures have taught it. It's traditional. Today we're dismantling the tradition.

Libby: If tradition started it, what started tradition?

'Isa: Human nature.

Libby: You mean conscience?

'Isa: Yes. Human *tradition* came from human *nature*, and human *conscience* is an essential part of human nature. Tradition is a public and external way of handing on the discoveries of that private, internal thing called "moral conscience". So throughout human history, pub-

35

lic tradition and private conscience have combined to teach moral absolutism.

Libby: I see. So you would call tradition "public conscience"?

'Isa: No, I would not. I would call it "public *teaching*", or "*training* in conscience". It's a thing that goes from some individuals—the teachers, especially parents—to other individuals—the students. Conscience exists only in individual human beings.

Libby: You're saying there's no such thing as a social conscience?

'Isa: Of course there is, but it exists in individuals.

Libby: So there's no . . . collective conscience?

'Isa: In a society of a hundred human beings, there are only one hundred consciences, not one hundred and one—because there are only one hundred souls there, not one hundred and one. "Society" is not another human being. It sounds like somebody; it sounds like a proper name, like Superman. But it isn't.

Libby: OK, Professor, but that sounds like a pretty abstract and technical point.

'Isa: It's a very practical point. It means that you can't blame society instead of individuals. You can only blame real people. "Collective responsibility" is a popular myth that gets you out of guilt, out of responsibility, and into the absurdity of blaming no individuals at all for the Holocaust, or slavery—just some ghost called the *Zeitgeist*, "the spirit of the times".

Libby: I see we're *not* avoiding controversial issues today, as I thought we would. I guess that's impossible for you. Let's get back to the main menu: Where do you think moral relativism came from? It must have come from history if it has a history, right? So it's not new.

'Isa: Of course. But the present is a radically new situation. What's new is the *level* of relativism among this society's intellectuals. And increasingly among their students, the masses.

Libby: Yet relativism has a history.

'Isa: Oh, yes. A long one, in fact.

Libby: How far back does it go?

'Isa: In *humanity's* history, it goes back to Eden.

Libby: "*Humanity's* history?" As distinct from . . . ?

'Isa: I mean the first relativist was not a human being but the Devil.

Libby: Why do you call the Devil a relativist?

'Isa: Listen to his philosophy: "Did God say that in the day you eat of the forbidden fruit you will die? I say you won't. God is keeping something from you. Eat this, and you will know what it is. You will know God's dark side. The light is relative to the dark, and the dark to the light. Good and evil are relative, you see."

Libby: That sounds pretty reasonable to me.

'Isa: See? That's how successful the Devil's advertising has been.

Libby: It's *advertising*?

'Isa: Yes, the world's oldest profession.

Libby: Seriously, Professor, what human *philosophers* invented relativism?

'Isa: The Sophists were the first that I know of.

Libby: As Plato portrays them.

'Isa: Yes. They were the dragons to dragonslayer Socrates.

Libby: How were they relativists? What, exactly, did they teach?

'Isa: The most famous was probably Protagoras, and his most famous saying was that "man is the measure of all things: of the goodness of things good and of the badness of things bad".

Libby: This was the Sophists' philosophy?

'Isa: This was their so-called wisdom. "Philosophy" means "the *love* of wisdom", the love of Sophia. The Sophists called themselves "wise men", men of Sophia. Socrates deliberately called himself only a *lover* of wisdom instead.

Libby: And why is this a crucial distinction?

'Isa: Because it shows how the arrogance of the Sophists naturally flows from their relativism, and the humility of Socrates naturally flows from his disagreement with relativism.

Libby: I don't see that. It seems to be exactly the opposite—to me, anyway, and to most people, I think. It's the absolutist who seems to be dogmatic and proud and who claims superior wisdom. The relativist tends to be a sceptic, and sceptics are humble, not dogmatic.

'Isa: That's exactly what your relativistic media has conditioned you to think. But look at it logically for once. Look at the defining slogan of Protagoras the Sophist: "Man is the measure of all things"—my mind, your mind, any individual human mind is the measure of all things, or at least of good and evil—what could be more arrogant than that?

Libby: Why do you call that arrogant?

'Isa: Because the *measurers* of wisdom can't be *measured* by wisdom, and so they can't be judged as unwise. If you are the measure, you are the God.

Libby: Of course we're not God . . .

'Isa: That's the Socratic humility speaking there—the humility Socrates expressed in preferring the title "philosopher", "lover of wisdom", courtier of Lady Wisdom, the goddess. You see? *That* implies that *God* is the measure of all things, and certainly of good and evil; that God is the measure of man, not man the measure of God. And since God is the measure of good and evil, we have moral absolutes. It's absolutism that's humble.

Libby: I see. That's a very different way of seeing things!

'Isa: It's different only because you've been hypnotized by the success of the Sophists' successors, your modern media propaganda.

Libby: So you claim the humble sceptic Socrates would be on your side in the relativism-absolutism debate.

'Isa: Absolutely! He was an absolutist, and his jihad, his holy struggle, was against the moral relativism of the Sophists. He fought for the true God against the idolatry of the human self. He was an intellectual warrior-saint.

Libby: But in all of Plato's dialogues he's the humble, sceptical one.

'Isa: My point exactly.

Libby: But that's not absolutism!

'Isa: Not if you *define* absolutism as arrogance. See what you're doing? You're confusing two different things: objective philosophy and subjective attitude; a sceptical philosophy and a humble attitude. The Sophists had a sceptical and relativist philosophy and an arrogant attitude. Socrates had an absolutist philosophy and a humble attitude.

Libby: Well, Socrates was an unusual combination. Most absolutists are arrogant, like you.

'Isa: Socrates was *not* unusual. *Most* religious people are humble because they know they're under God. But they're absolutists because their principles come from God. You see? Their humility and their absolutism come from the same source. It's not an unusual combination at all; it's inevitable. God, therefore absolutism. *Under* God, therefore humble.

Libby: Well, I'm not here to argue today, but to interview, so I'll let that go.

'Isa: You mean you can't refute it so you'll let it go.

Libby: I mean I'll ignore your insults and continue doing my job. Where did relativism pop up next in history?

'Isa: In the philosophers of Plato's Later Academy. That's ironic, because Plato was Socrates' faithful disciple. But after Plato's death, his successors in the Academy became sceptics. In fact, they were so famous for their scepticism that the word *academic* became synonymous with *sceptic* in the ancient world. When Augustine wrote his dialogue against the sceptics, he called it "Against the Academics".

Libby: Were there other relativists in ancient philosophy?

'Isa: Oh, yes. The Epicureans. They were materialists and hedonists.

Libby: And were there absolutists who opposed them too?

'Isa: Yes, mainly the Stoics, and the Aristotelians, and the Neo-Platonists.

Libby: And were there relativists in medieval philosophy too?

'Isa: Very few. Most Islamic and Jewish and Christian philosophers were too religious to let that camel under the tent. But you might see

Averroes as a Muslim relativist with his notion of one truth for the philosophers and a different truth for the masses. And Peter Abelard was a sort of Christian relativist with his new teaching that your personal, subjective motive was the defining thing that made any act good or evil. But the main foundation for modern relativism in medieval Christian philosophy was William of Ockham's Nominalism. Nominalism was the philosophy that reduced all universal terms to mere names, *nomina*—there are no *real* universals, is what Nominalism says —and therefore there are no real *moral* universals, like "honesty is always good" or "adultery is always evil", by the very nature of those things, by their unchangeable essence.

Libby: So Ockham thought good and evil depended on the changing situation? Or the subjective motive? Or what?

'Isa: No, actually he said it depended on God's will. So he wasn't really a moral relativist himself. But "Ockham's Razor" was his famous principle that *led* to relativism. That's the principle that a philosopher should "never multiply entities beyond necessity", that is, you should always choose the simplest hypothesis, the most reductionistic explanation. Reduce the complex to the simple. That's why he eliminated universals.

Libby: You're losing me. Could you be more specific? What would be some examples of Ockham's Razor? How would it be used?

'Isa: Suppose you're trying to explain the rise of Nazism in Germany. One hypothesis might use angels and demons and occult supernatural forces; the other hypothesis would use only visible, human forces: economic depression, resentment at losing World War I, and so on. Or suppose you're trying to explain schizophrenia. One hypothesis might bring in the soul, and another hypothesis would bring in only the brain.

Libby: And Ockham's Razor says to explain things by the minimum number of causes.

'Isa: Right.

Libby: And that's relativism?

'Isa: No, but it gave birth to relativism.

Libby: How?

'Isa: First, through what philosophers today call the "divine command theory". Luther and Calvin and Descartes followed Ockham there; their "divine command theory" got rid of the more complex natural law theory. The divine command theory says that God's command is the only thing that makes an act right, or morally good. The natural law theory says that there is also a natural law, as well as a divine law—a law that comes from the nature of the act itself, and the nature of man, and that this natural law also makes an act good or evil. The natural law is the proximate cause; the divine law is the ultimate cause. Two causes instead of one: not the *simplest* explanation.

Libby: I don't understand. Wouldn't the Razor want to eliminate religion? So why would a Razor man choose the divine command theory?

'Isa: It could work either way. The Razor could be used to eliminate the natural law *or* the divine law. The religious Nominalists like Luther thought they could maximize religion by eliminating the natural law, and the nonreligious Nominalists thought they could minimize religion by eliminating the divine law. Both sides used the Razor. The same principle that the Protestant reformers used to eliminate the natural law and the natural human reason that knows it, the *secularists* used to eliminate *divine* law and the faith that knows that. So faith and reason became enemies instead of the allies that they were in all classical medieval philosophy, whether Islamic or Jewish or Christian. Islamic philosophy had had the same controversy centuries earlier.

Libby: And this question—the question of the role of the divine command in making an act right or wrong—this question goes back to Socrates, doesn't it?

'Isa: Yes. In the *Euthyphro* he asks the key question . . .

Libby: Is a thing right because God wills it, or does God will it because it's right? I remember.

'Isa: I'll give you an A minus for that.

Libby: Only an A minus?

'Isa: What Socrates actually said was: Is a thing pious because it is loved by the gods, or is it loved by the gods because it is pious?

Libby: "Pious", "right", "good"—it comes to pretty much the same thing, doesn't it?

'Isa: Yes, except that *pious* is a religious word and brings in a relationship to God or gods, while *good* and *right* might not. But the important difference is between *God* and *gods* . . .

Libby: Why?

'Isa: Because if there are many gods, Socrates can win the argument easily, because what one god loves, another god may hate, so if *good* means only "loved by gods", as Euthyphro says, then the same act becomes both good and evil at the same time, which is a contradiction. Socrates reduces Euthyphro to absurdity this way. But if there's only one God, if "there is no God but God", then that absurdity disappears. But then another problem appears . . .

Libby: Go on.

'Isa: There's this dilemma, you see: What is the *relation* between the intrinsic goodness of an act and God willing it, or between the intrinsic natural badness of an act and God forbidding it? Which is the cause of the other? If God's law causes an act to be good or evil, then God seems arbitrary and irrational, and we're back in pagan theology with Zeus instead of God—one arbitrary, irrational despot instead of thousands, but nevertheless a despot. That's the bad *religious* consequence. The bad *human* consequence is that all of human morality then seems to come from God's mere power, not from anything rational, anything our reason can understand. (Assuming we can't understand God's mind and motives, only our own.) That's the first horn of the dilemma. The other horn is this: if you say the causality works the other way round, if you say that the nature of the human act is the cause or reason why God wills it or forbids it, then you're putting something above God. Because you're saying that this thing —the intrinsic nature of the human act—is the *cause* of God willing it. And then God is no longer God, no longer the First Cause, the Uncaused Cause. So you're back in pagan theology again.

Libby: Whew! How do *you* escape that dilemma?

'Isa: I thought we were supposed to be talking about the history of moral relativism, not about me.

Libby: Are you weaseling out of the hard question?

'Isa: No, I have an answer.

Libby: Well?

'Isa: It's both. That's where Ockham's Razor is wrong. An act is good or evil both because of its nature *and* because of God's will. And God's will is rational, not arbitrary, because it flows from his nature. He *is* good. That's why he *wills* good for us, and that's why good acts are good. So there are really *three* things involved, three causes, in a sense: God's nature, God's will, and the nature of the act. The Razor tempts you to cut two of them away.

Libby: But if you need all three, wouldn't the Razor still work? Because it says to eliminate *unnecessary* complexity, but not necessary complexity. And your argument just proved that these three causes were all necessary. So the Razor is still a good principle, if you use it right. It eliminates only things like leprechauns.

'Isa: Fine; if you want to rehabilitate Ockham, that's not my concern. The dragon I'm after is not the Razor but relativism. I just think the use, or misuse, of the Razor is a major historical cause of relativism.

Libby: So you think the Razor was applied to the neck instead of the hair?

'Isa: Nicely put.

Libby: Why, thank you, Professor. Do I get my A now?

'Isa: Only if you act like a good little reporter.

Libby: I shall meekly submit. What came next in your story of the rise of relativism, then?

'Isa: The so-called Enlightenment in the West—though I would call it the "Endarkenment". The Enlightenment was essentially rationalism, the exaltation of reason over faith as absolute—in Descartes, for instance. Then, in reaction against that, Empiricism, which replaced *reason* with *sensation* as the only trustworthy way to certainty. And in the nineteenth century Romanticism replaced reason with *emotion*.

Libby: What did Empiricism have to do with moral relativism?

'**Isa:** Empiricism led to what's called the "emotivist theory of value": the notion that moral judgments like "murder is wrong" are really only expressions of the speaker's subjective feelings about murder rather than statements about the real, objective nature of the act of murder—in other words, that "there's nothing right or wrong, but thinking makes it so".

Libby: And why do you think this stemmed from *Empiricism*?

'**Isa:** Because we don't *see* moral goodness or evil with our eyes or hear it with our ears. It doesn't register on any of our physical senses. So if you're an Empiricist, and you reduce all knowledge of objective reality to sense knowledge, where do you put morality then? If it's not *sensory*, it's not *objective*, not objectively real, not any knowledge of objective reality. So it must be subjective, in us, from us, relative to us. The emotivist theory says it's our *feelings*.

Libby: That answer was supplied by Romanticism, I suppose.

'**Isa:** Yes.

Libby: Which philosopher first invented the emotivist theory of values?

'**Isa:** David Hume is probably the key philosopher here. He's the Empiricist who analyzed moral judgments as subjective feelings. "Murder is evil" really means "I hate murder".

Libby: Hume was eighteenth century, right? How does this get into the twentieth century?

'**Isa:** The most influential philosophy in the twentieth century in English-speaking countries was Logical Positivism, and then Analytic Philosophy, its child, and Hume was their hero.

Libby: Why?

'**Isa:** Because he got rid of God for them, you see. Analytic Philosophy was a kind of secular Humeanism.

Libby: Could we have some philosophy instead of puns, Professor?

'**Isa:** How *serious* you people are!

Libby: "You people?" Which of the many oppressed classes that I represent is the one you're trying to insult now? Is it women, or Blacks, or liberals?

'Isa: Actually, I was thinking of reporters! I'm sorry. Let's do just what you said and get back to philosophy.

Libby: Hmmph!

'Isa: Analytic philosophy has an axiom, an assumption—they almost always accept this as a truism—that there's a radical distinction between *facts* and *values*. Facts are objective, and values are not. And this truism—this false truism of professional philosophy—has seeped out into popular thinking by a kind of osmosis. It comes out in our use of the word *values* instead of *laws* or *virtues* or *goods*. *Nobody* ever used the word *values* to refer to anything moral or ethical before the nineteenth century, before . . . Nietzsche, I think, or maybe it goes back to Kant, I'm not sure, but certainly not before Kant. No one in the eighteenth century or any other time before that would have understood the stupid saying everybody says today: "Don't impose your values on me."

Libby: Are you saying Kant was to blame for this? Are you labeling Kant a relativist now?

'Isa: No, Kant was not a moral relativist. But I think he has to shoulder a lot of the blame for it. He tried to defend morality against Hume, but he gave up too much. He tried to defend the *universality* and *necessity* of moral judgments by giving up their *objectivity*.

Libby: Their *what*?

'Isa: I guess I'd better do some more translating here. OK, let's see . . . a judgment is *universal* if it's *always* true, and *necessary* if it *has* to be true. There can't be any exceptions to it in any time or place. Kant wanted to defend that part of traditional morality. Traditional morality said that some acts were always wrong, for everybody, in all situations and all times. But traditional morality also said that moral judgments were *objectively* true, that they told you something about objective reality, about the nature of things out there, independent of our minds and our opinions.

Libby: How could "values" be "out there" like atoms?

'**Isa:** Ah, that's the point, that's the big difference. Traditional philosophy had a bigger conception of the "out there", a deeper world view. You see, "out there" didn't mean just matter to them; it had a spiritual dimension too, a moral dimension. So the goodness or badness of some acts was part of objective reality, according to . . . well, according to *all* cultures before the so-called Enlightenment. It's really a difference in metaphysics, this difference between moral relativism and absolutism. The absolutist says reality includes things like God or gods, and angels, or spirits. And eternal truths, the nature of things, unchangeable essences, Platonic Ideas, divine Ideas. So reality can include objective values, real goods. Morality was a dimension of *reality* before the Enlightenment, not just a dimension of our thinking or feeling.

Libby: That's a matter of metaphysics, then. "Dimensions of reality" —that sounds pretty abstract to most people. Can you be more concrete? What difference do you think that old metaphysics made to morality?

'**Isa:** It gave us an objective standard for morality. And that's the only reason our opinions about it can ever be wrong: there's an objective standard.

Libby: Ah, you mean it justified judgmentalism.

'**Isa:** That's exactly right. If it's not objectively real—if morality's not objectively real—then nothing can be really morally wrong. Then no one should be "judgmental" and "impose" his own personal, subjective values on others. Because that's all values are then: private, personal, subjective.

Libby: No, they can still be public, collective, social.

'**Isa:** OK, but where did they come from?

Libby: From consensus, or cooperation.

'**Isa:** Right. That is, from man's will.

Libby: And woman's!

'**Isa:** And what is consensus? It means a majority of the individuals in a society coming together and agreeing to make *their* values into laws, or "society's standards".

Libby: Right. So?

'Isa: So this: a law is enforced only by force. So your "consensus" really means that *some* individuals—the lawmakers, whoever they are —the majority in a democracy—impose *their* personal values, their will, on the others! *That's* "judgmentalism", that's imposition. But if morality is objective instead of subjective, if it comes from universal human nature instead of some human wills, then that's *not* "judgmentalism", not an imposition at all. It's exactly the opposite of what the relativist says. The relativist is accusing the *absolutist* of exactly the moral fault *he's* guilty of. What a piece of propaganda! And it's worked! It's become the prevailing view, as you said—my view seems strange, and yours seems normal. It worked because it's a big lie instead of a little one. Don't you see that, Libby? Don't you see the *hypocrisy* of it? It's not just bad philosophy. It's bad morality; it's hypocrisy; it's dishonest. The very people who say, "Don't impose your values on me because they're only relative and subjective" then go on to create a society that they say is only man-made, not based on God or natural law, and they say that all values come from man, so a society is then nothing but some men imposing *their* values on others—majorities on minorities, or rulers on ruled, or teachers on students, or media mind molders on the stupid, traditionalist masses.

Libby: How could people be so stupid, if your scenario is true? Why did this big lie, if that's what it is, why did it work? Where did it begin?

'Isa: It begins in the schools, the state propaganda machines that propagandize this moral relativism into the students from kindergarten through graduate school, and they call this propaganda "values clarification" courses.

Libby: What a fascinating hypothesis!

'Isa: It's not a hypothesis. It's a hypocrisy. Because these relativists turn out to be not relativistic at all about one thing: their relativism. That's their one nonnegotiable absolute.

Libby: Really?

'Isa: No, there's usually one other one: abortion. I never heard of a prolife relativist. All good "liberals" *have* to pass the litmus test and support their society's Holocaust. And that's another big lie: that it's somehow "liberal" to crush a baby's skull. Can't you see it? The very language shows the hypocrisy. Relativism's not just a philosophy, because a philosophy is rational and open to reason. It's their creed, their faith, their religion. Or their love, or their lover. In fact, it's usually their excuse for *having* a lover.

Libby: My, my, we certainly have wandered far from our objective, scientific analysis of the history of Western philosophy, Professor . . . or shall I call you the Prophet?

'Isa: Careful! There may really be such a thing as blasphemy, if all values aren't relative.

Libby: I think you were talking about Kant when you fell into your prophetic trance. Could we get back to the history of philosophy now?

'Isa: Hmph! All right. Where were we in Kant?

Libby: How was he a cause of relativism if he wasn't a relativist? He was a traditionalist in morality, wasn't he?

'Isa: No. He was a revolutionary. He knew he was a revolutionary. He called his most important idea his "Copernican revolution in philosophy". That was the notion that the human mind *makes* the truth instead of *discovering* it, that truth is formed by the human mind. And that includes moral truth. Kant called true morality "autonomous", that is, man-made rather than "heteronomous", made by another, by God. So *our* will makes the moral law, not God's. We make it; we don't discover it. I'd call that subjectivism. It's nine-tenths of the way to moral relativism. It's not yet moral relativism because Kant also believed that all minds necessarily worked the same way and created the same morality—like logic or math. So morality was *universal* and *necessary* for Kant but not *objective*. But that's only one short step from relativism.

Libby: Why?

'Isa: Because if morality is mine, if I made it up, it's hard to see why I can't remake it or unmake it when I want to. And at some point I'll certainly try to, to get rid of guilt and judgment. Kant tried to prevent that, but he failed. He tried to prevent it by arguing that I can't logically succeed in creating my own morality contrary to the universal Golden Rule, and absolute "Categorical Imperative". It's logically inconsistent to will that everyone lie or steal when I do. But he failed because why should I care about logic if I made that up too? The logic I made tells me that I can't unmake it, and the morality that I made tells me that I can't unmake it—well, why should the father obey the child? Why shouldn't Doctor Frankenstein reprogram his monster, or tame it, or kill it, if he wants to? It's *his* invention, after all.

Libby: And who is next on your hit list after Kant?

'Isa: Hegel. Hegel was Kant's ghost buster. The ghost he busted was the little remaining ghost of objective reality that Kant still admitted. Kant called it "things in themselves". He believed this was something real but unknowable. Hegel argued: if it's unknowable, if we can't know it, then how can you know it's there? Knowing the unknowable enough to know it exists—that's a self-contradiction. Kant tried to limit thought, to draw a border to thought; but to do that, you have to *think* both sides of the border.

Libby: "To draw a limit to thought, thought must think both sides of the limit"—I learned that line in Wittgenstein. (See? I can rhyme!)

'Isa: Wittgenstein must have got it from Hegel. Actually, Hegel got the argument from Fichte.

Libby: Professor, I don't think most people care about all those names . . .

'Isa: Right. But I think they do care about this idea from Hegel: Hegel added another idea that became a part of relativism: universal process. Everything flows; everything is in flux. Truth itself evolves, even God evolves, through human history, according to Hegel. So there's another reason to believe that everything is relative, relative to the stage of development.

Libby: Even God evolves, according to Hegel?

'Isa: Yes. History is like a mother, and God is its baby.

Libby: And?

'Isa: And then along came Nietzsche, who aborted the baby. Or rather, who claimed that the baby was already aborted. "God is dead."

Nietzsche was an Existentialist, and Existentialism was a reaction against Hegel, but it was usually even more relativistic than Hegel.

Libby: Can you generalize about Existentialists? They're a very mixed bag, aren't they?

'Isa: Yes, but one of the few ideas they all hold is their rejection of "abstractions"—that is, universals, including moral universals.

Libby: Even the religious Existentialists? Even Kierkegaard?

'Isa: Yes. In *Fear and Trembling* Kierkegaard praises Abraham for transcending the moral law when he was willing to kill Isaac because "the individual is higher than the universal". There were a lot of different philosophies that arose in the nineteenth century, and most of them were reactions against Hegel, and just about all of them were more relativistic. Pragmatism, for instance, explicitly rejects absolutes, especially moral absolutes, absolute ends. And Positivism is essentially the reduction of everything to the "positive scientific".

Libby: What does that mean?

'Isa: There are different kinds of Positivism, but all of them reject the natural moral law. The only law they accept is "positive law", not natural law: the law posited by man, made by man. That's true in Comte—you could call him a metaphysical positivist—and in Ayer, the Logical Positivist, and in Marx—you could call Marxism "historical positivism"—and the linguistic positivism of the early Wittgenstein.

Libby: And all this is still the reigning philosophy today?

'Isa: More than that, even: it's the law! Moral positivism is now the official philosophy of the United States of America. The Supreme Court said so, in *Planned Parenthood v. Casey*. They explicitly repudiated the appeal to a natural moral law. That was an even more radical decision than *Roe v. Wade*, because *Roe v. Wade* only legalized killing unborn human beings on the basis that a few Supreme Court justices claimed that they knew that nobody knew whether human babies were human or not. But *Casey* established the positivist premise that can justify *any* immoral conclusion: abortion and sodomy today, infanticide and suicide tomorrow, necrophilia, bestiality, incest, and cannibalism next year, or whenever Hollywood decrees our next moral conversion.

Libby: I see you're waxing prophetic again, Professor. But I won't comment on that. What about *philosophy* today?

'Isa: The most fashionable philosophy in American universities today is Deconstructionism, and that's the explicit denial of the very essence of language: "intentionality". That's the technical, traditional term for the quality words have that makes them meaningful, significant, *signs* that point beyond themselves to objective reality. There is no objective reality to these Deconstructionists, no world beyond texts. Texts are worlds, and worlds are texts.

Libby: And what does that have to do with morality?

'Isa: It makes morality as arbitrary as penmanship.

Libby: Can you be more specific? Who's the number one Deconstructionist?

'Isa: No one. They're all little philosophers. But their favorite great philosopher is Nietzsche. Nietzsche was really the first Deconstructionist. He called himself "the philosopher with a hammer". The destroyer. Especially in language. He said, "We—that is, we atheists—have not gotten rid of God until we have gotten rid of grammar." You see, grammar is the traces of God and creation and form and objective truth and order in language. So the Deconstructionists rage against even that trace of divine order, because they see it's connected with moral order. Nietzsche himself let the cat out of the bag when he said, "To understand a philosopher's metaphysics, look at the morality it leads to."

Libby: And what morality does Deconstructionism lead to?

'Isa: Let's look. DeMan was a Nazi liar. Foucault was a sadomasochistic sodomite. Look at the philosophers they love: the Marquis de Sade, a demon-possessed Satanist, perhaps the most purely evil man who ever lived.

Libby: I have a tiny little sneaking suspicion you have a few tiny reservations about Deconstructionism, to put it mildly. And putting it mildly is what we're increasingly not doing.

'Isa: Why should we? When you're confronted with an evil, perverted, nasty little kid smashing a chandelier with a hammer, why should you use gentleman's language? It's decadence; it's death wish; it's necrophilia; it's the end of sanity and civilization.

Libby: Professor, I think we'd better stop for this morning. I don't want you to boil over like an apoplectic kettle.

'Isa: No, of course not. That wouldn't be polite, would it?—to sound a harsh alarm in the middle of a plague. All right, let's pick up the pieces tonight.

Libby: Whew! And to think I thought this session was going to be easy and noncontroversial!

Interview 4

The Data

Libby: Professor, when we set up these interviews, you said you thought we needed one whole interview just on *data*. And that's tonight's agenda. That sounds very scientific. Do you think we can solve this problem of whether there are moral absolutes by the scientific method? Or is it strictly a question for philosophy?

'Isa: It's not either/or. Philosophy is scientific too, though it's not a laboratory science or a mathematical science.

Libby: How is it a science, then? It doesn't use the scientific method.

'Isa: Yes it does. The scientific method in the broadest sense means first of all assuming that reality is rational and intelligible—the ancient pagans didn't assume that, and the modern nihilist doesn't either, so it's not automatic—and then, in the second place, assuming that human reason can know it (those are two assumptions that much of modern philosophy is sceptical of, by the way); and then, third, demanding that we have to give good reasons, or evidence, for our conclusions; and then, in the fourth place, stipulating that good evidence means that our theories have to be controlled by our data, not vice versa. The data justify the theory: the theory that explains the data best wins. It doesn't have to be *empirical* data, but it has to be *data*, something given to all of us, something anyone can experience as given to him rather than invented by him. (The very word *data* means "given.")

Libby: That's why you think it's important to take a whole interview on the data, to get our data straight before we argue theory?

'Isa: Exactly. That's one of the reasons I hate Deconstructionism so much: it denies that basic principle of "first data, then interpretation; data controls interpretation". They reverse the order.

Libby: But that reversal isn't new, is it? Don't we all color our data by our interpretation? It's not easy to be totally objective. Maybe it's not even possible.

'Isa: But that's always been recognized as a *temptation*, not justified as a whole philosophy.

Libby: How do you know that's not all we can do? How do you know we *can* be objective?

'Isa: If you don't at least try to be objective, you'll never know because you'll never have the data. All I want to do is to *try* at least to be what working people call "honest"—as in "an honest day's work"—and what working scientists call "objective". I don't claim I will be 100% successful.

Libby: I'm thrilled to hear you admit that, Professor. I find that the most refreshing thing you've said yet.

'Isa: That may reveal an interesting fact about your psyche, Libby, but it does not help us to find and define our data—which is what we are supposed to be about in this interview, isn't it?

Libby: I thought it was about *your* psyche . . . but let that pass. Where do you look for data when you want to find out whether there are moral absolutes or not?

'Isa: That's an important question. One of the Logical Positivists' strongest objections to traditional philosophy was that it had no data, as the "positive sciences" did. And I think that objection is in the minds of a lot of people who are sceptical of philosophy, sceptical of the power of philosophy to solve anything or settle anything or prove anything with certainty.

Libby: And what's your answer to the objection?

'Isa: Very simply, philosophy *has* data: it's ordinary experience.

Libby: That's "phenomenology", isn't it?

'Isa: I don't want to worry about technical terms, but basically yes.

Libby: So you want to find some moral experience as your data. So where do you look?

'Isa: I think we have to include at least four distinguishable levels, or circles, or horizons of moral experience that we all have. Most immediately, there's personal, individual moral experience. The three most basic moral terms—*good* and *right* and *ought*—all come from there. They're meaningful to everybody . . .

Libby: Could you take the time to show us that in a little detail before going on to the other three levels?

'Isa: Yes. Those three words come from three moral experiences that we all have. First, we all experience some things as not only *desired* but *desirable*—as really *good* because of what they are and because of what we are. We really need things like knowledge and health and friends. So there's *good*.

Then there's *right*. We all experience some deeds as the *right* thing to do and others as *wrong*. Some things just aren't just, or fair, or right. Even very small children know that. We also know intuitively that people have "rights"—ourselves and others. It's not right to kill you because you have a right to life. It's not right to steal your money because you have a right to your own property.

And then there's *ought*. We all experience being morally *obligated* to do some things and avoid others.

Libby: That's "conscience", right?

'Isa: *Conscience* is the word we use for that faculty of our soul, or our psyche—the faculty that . . . well, actually conscience does *three* things: it *informs* you that you really ought to do good and avoid doing evil (and it also informs you about what things are good and what things are evil); and it also *moves* you or gently pushes you to do good and avoid evil; and then it makes you feel guilty if you choose evil instead of good. So it works on your intellect *and* your will *and* your feelings. So ordinary moral experience of goodness and rightness and oughtness is our data.

Libby: That's private data, though.

'Isa: But everyone has it.

Libby: But you have no public, observable data, do you?

'Isa: Yes, we do. That's the second level of data: interpersonal moral behavior, how we treat each other.

Libby: But how we *do* treat each other is only facts, empirical facts. How we feel we *ought* to treat each other is moral values. But that's not public, observable data. Animals see how we treat each other too, but they don't have any moral sense. How can morality be something you can see as data?

'Isa: You're assuming the radical distinction between facts and values that we saw this morning coming from Logical Positivism, and leading right to moral relativism. I deny that assumption. Values are facts too!

Libby: Where do they show up in the public, observable data, then?

'Isa: In data like . . . *quarrelling*, not just fighting but quarrelling, arguing about right and wrong, about who's right and who has rights. And *praising* other people for doing something right, and *blaming* them for doing wrong. Animals don't do that. And also the experience of *receiving* praise or blame—not just "conditioning", animal training, but moral praise or blame. And also *commanding* someone to do right and commanding them to stop doing wrong. You don't issue commands to a machine. A command assumes the free will to obey or disobey. You don't really command animals either. You condition them; you train them. And the other side of that experience too, *being commanded* to do right and avoid wrong. And *counseling* or advising someone to do right, and avoid wrong, and *being counseled*. And *rewarding and punishing*, and *being* rewarded or punished. Not just conditioning, now, not just "I'm going to give you pain until you stop doing x", but "I'm going to punish you for doing x because x is wrong and you deserve to be punished." It's *justice*, not just power or success. Do you see the difference? Between animal experience and human moral experience? I think I mentioned seventeen differences there, seventeen moral things, moral experiences, distinctively human experiences, not shared by machines or plants or even animals.

Libby: Psychologists will disagree with you there, I think.

'Isa: Some will. Some won't. The commonsensical ones won't, the human ones.

Libby: I see: whoever disagrees with you isn't human.

'Isa: You know that's not what I meant.

Libby: Yes, but it's great fun to defuse the bomb you threw at me this morning about "how *serious* you people are".

'Isa: Touché, Libby. Now can we get back to the point?

Libby: You mean your lecture?

'Isa: My answer to your questions.

Libby: And my question now is this: Can you prove the psychologists are wrong when they say we're just clever animals? Can you prove there's a difference in kind?

'Isa: We all know these seventeen pieces of moral data from experience. We have moral experiences. If there's no difference in kind between us and the animals, then the animals must be moral agents too. I guess we don't know for sure that animals are *not* moral, but we do know for sure that we are. We can't get inside their minds, but we can get inside ours—unless we're professional psychologists! They're the only ones who doubt that we're moral agents and think we're the same as animals.

Libby: So everybody's sane except the psychologists?

'Isa: The ones who deny free will and moral responsibility and think we're just animals with bigger brains, yes. Every ordinary human being knows better than that. There are some ideas that are just so stupid that only a Ph.D. can believe them.

Libby: You're pretty down on psychologists.

'Isa: Not all of them. I said that before: some do, some don't deny our humanity. But some just don't see what we all see—or maybe they see it but they just choose not to believe it, like a Buddhist who doesn't believe that matter is real, even though he sees it.

Libby: I think a psychologist would reply that you're asking a metaphysical question here, about what's ultimately real, while they're only scientists who try to explain connections between phenomena, causes and effects, and the only scientific phenomenon here is human behavior. That's our only data. The rest is theory: free will, and responsibility, and conscience, and morality.

'Isa: No, that's data too, primary data. We all know it from experience, not theory. *Empiricism* is the theory, the "ism". Confining experience to sense experience is the theory.

Libby: Well, they wouldn't admit that. Moral experience isn't observable *behavior*.

'Isa: But it *causes* behavior, or inhibits behavior—it makes a difference to behavior.

Libby: According to your theory. But not theirs.

'Isa: No, it's not a matter of theory; it's a matter of data, if you only look. Look within. That's data too. And it affects visible behavior. When you disobey your conscience, you behave differently. When you ignore your moral experience, your visible experience changes. You go out and kill people. But you can't kill people without killing conscience first.

Libby: That still seems like private data—conscience. And the connection between conscience and behavior—that's not visible. Only the behavior is.

'Isa: But we can experience the fact that conscience makes a difference to our behavior.

Libby: But that experience—the experience of the connection between the inner conscience and the outer act—is just as invisible as the invisible inner experience itself. Give me something totally public.

'Isa: All right, here's a third level of moral data: moral language, public moral discourse.

Libby: Words are data? Like in a dictionary?

'Isa: No, the *meaning* of the moral words, the fact that we understand those meanings. The seventeen moral experiences we went through —they correspond to seventeen words, and each of those words has meaning. We all understand those meanings. And that's data. You see, ordinary language contains a wealth of meaning. Philosophers "unpack" it and examine it. That was the data Socrates always explored. And it was mainly moral questions—in fact, it was always moral questions—that he explored. Here's the father of philosophy, the first philosopher, and he has plenty of data, and he has the right philosophical method in place already: the logical analysis of ordinary language.

Libby: How can *words* be *data*?

'Isa: Because they come from ordinary experience. They're like fossils of experience.

Libby: Oh. That makes sense. Hmm . . . didn't you say there were *four* levels of data? We've got three so far, by my count: individual moral experience, interpersonal moral behavior, and public moral language.

'Isa: Right. The fourth would be human history . . .

Libby: You mean what we've learned from the follies of the past?

'Isa: That too, but I was thinking first of all of the *wisdom* of the past. Moral tradition. Tradition as a kind of collective moral memory. Most of our moral instruction comes from that source, I think.

Libby: You think it comes from tradition more than from experience?

'Isa: Tradition *is* experience: experience expanded beyond the narrow confines of the individual and the present. Chesterton called tradition "the democracy of the dead".

Libby: Oh—but of course that's not a universally accepted norm any more. Tradition, I mean. In fact, the idea that the past is somehow normative is probably the one feature that most distinguishes premodern societies from modern societies. Tradition still exists, of course, I grant you, but it doesn't bind us any more. Most of us are emancipated from tradition today.

'Isa: And from morality!

Libby: Perhaps you have a point there, a half truth, anyway. We may have sacrificed morality for success.

'Isa: But morality *is* the secret of success for a society, and tradition gives you morality, so tradition is the secret of social success. You can see that empirically, in history. Those societies that were the most traditional were also the most moral and the most successful. The three societies that lasted the longest, the three most successful societies in human history, and the most just and peaceful ones, were all founded by moralists who established a tradition that their societies kept faithfully. I mean Moses, Confucius, and Muhammad. Mosaic tradition is still alive after almost 4,000 years, in Christianity as well as Judaism; and Confucianism lasted 2,000 years; and Islam is still growing after almost 1,500 years. These are the world's richest databases, or data banks for morality.

Libby: But each society is different; you can't just clone the ideal society. We can learn a bit from every one, I guess, but each society's tradition can have only a limited relevance to other societies. America, for instance, is not a Mosaic or a Confucian or an Islamic society.

'Isa: No, and it's decaying fast because it isn't—because it has no roots, no moral tradition.

Libby: Do you really think that *that's* the key to being moral, that's the most important thing you need: just don't change the past?

'Isa: No, obviously you need much more than that. But . . .

Libby: Well, do you think America is becoming immoral because it's not traditional? Is that the main reason?

'Isa: I think the main reason is because of the decay of the family. That's the one absolutely essential building block of any human society. And "family" means "tradition". Families are what carry on tradition, from one generation to another. "Generation"—that's a family word. Once the "generation gap" widens enough, society slips through the cracks. Good-bye.

Libby: Hmmm—let's see if we can find our way back to our agenda now. Data—you say we have four areas of moral data, or moral experience: individual moral experience, interpersonal behavior, moral language, and historical tradition, right?

'Isa: Right.

Libby: Well, what do we do with that data now? How do we move from data to proof? How do your moral data prove moral absolutism?

'Isa: I'll give you one proof tonight, and more tomorrow or whenever we're scheduled to cover that. But I want to do this one tonight because it's the one that's the closest to the data. That's why it's the strongest and simplest and most obvious of all arguments for moral absolutism. In fact, it's so strong that it doesn't seem like an argument at all; it seems like an unnatural strain to put it into the form of a logical argument. It's almost the data itself.

Libby: What is it?

'Isa: The fact that the first and foundational moral experience we have is always absolutistic. Only later do you get relativism—later in the life of the individual or of the society. Sophistication sometimes suggests changing to relativism. But we can all remember what moral experience was like before we became sophisticated. It was absolute. We bumped up against moral law like a wall. That's why little kids are always so "black and white".

Libby: They're simplistic. When we mature, we grow out of that. (Some of us, anyway.) Are you saying we shouldn't?

'Isa: Whether we *should* or not is something to argue about. But the data, the fact, is that we always do begin as absolutists; we give absolute meanings to "good and evil", "right and wrong", "should and shouldn't".

Libby: That doesn't prove we were *right* when we were so simplistic. If *that's* your argument, boy, you're *really* simplistic!

'Isa: No, my argument is that the data comes first, the experience comes first, and it has to judge the theory, not vice versa. That's just good scientific method. Real, objective morality—absolute morality —can be denied by your modern theory, but only after it is first affirmed by your natural moral experience, by everybody's moral experience. You can deny moral absolutes only as a Buddhist denies matter.

Libby: You used that analogy before. I don't understand that—your correlation between morality and matter. What do they have in common?

'Isa: They're both immediate: conscience immediately detects real right and wrong, just as the senses immediately detect real colors and shapes. Then, later, your theory might tell you to mistrust your experience. Your guru may tell you that "your eyes deceive you; that elephant isn't really there; stop running. Don't be afraid of death; the body is an illusion." Moral relativism is like that. It denies the data. Moral relativism is to moral experience what Buddhism is to the experience of the senses, or what Mary Baker Eddy's "Christian Science" is to the experience of sickness and death. These philosophies all tell us not to trust our experience, that our experience deceives us, that the thing we experience isn't really there! They say the experience is an illusion to be overcome by faith. You see? Moral relativism is a faith, a dogma, an ideology. Moral absolutism is empirical, or experiential. It's data based, data friendly.

Libby: And modern psychology isn't data friendly, isn't scientific? You're saying that ancient absolutism is more scientific than modern psychology?

'Isa: Yes indeed! Modern psychology—very modern psychology, very secular, very liberal psychology—tells you that all those moral words —"should" and "ought" and "right" and "wrong"—are "mistakes"! I just read a book the other day about "the ten fundamental psychological mistakes". One of them was "making 'should-statements' ". In other words, there's only one thing really wrong: thinking anything is really wrong! Immorality isn't forbidden any more; morality is!

Libby: Sounds to me like you're just venting, not being scientific. Prove to me that moral absolutism is true from the data. Give me something concrete.

'Isa: I will if you only look at the data. Look! On all levels of data —individual and family and neighborhood and nation and world— you experience desires, and you also experience conscience telling you what desires are right and what desires are wrong. A nation has a desire to steal the land of another nation, but there's a peace treaty, so it's wrong to go to war to take the land. We always experience those two levels: what is and what ought to be. "What is" includes things like our nation's tiny bit of land and the other nation's great big piece of it. And also the fact that we covet more land. That's a fact too, a psychological fact. It *is*. But we experience more than "what *is*" as our data; we also experience "what *ought to be*" as part of our data. We experience conscience telling us that it's wrong to covet that land or to steal it, or to go to war for it, because we have no right to it;

it is not right. And that dimension of right and wrong, that's just as much a part of our experienced data as the land and our desire for it.

Libby: But the land is out there, and you can verify it with your senses.

'Isa: And your desire for the land is not out there. It's in you. And it has no color. You can't sense it. But you can verify it; you can know it just as you can know the land. It's immediate.

Libby: OK, that's true of your desires, but it's not true of the value you place on your desires. The moral dimension isn't immediate data like that. It's an interpretation of the data.

'Isa: No it isn't. That's my whole point. The data about what's right and wrong comes to us just as immediately as the data about the facts of land and the facts of our desire.

Libby: So there aren't two dimensions, then, but only one: the immediate?

'Isa: No, there are two: what is and what ought to be. But they're both data, both immediate. Just as we have immediate color detectors—eyes—and immediate desire detectors—self-awareness—we also have immediate good-and-evil detectors—consciences. They're all part of our data.

Libby: So how does this prove moral absolutism is true?

'Isa: It shows that absolutism is scientific. It's true to the data, the experience. Moral experience does not come to us in relative colors. We get moral relativism from later relativistic philosophers; we get moral absolutism from moral experience. The argument is that only moral absolutism is true to the data.

Libby: I guess either you just see it or you don't.

'Isa: No, I think you don't *let* yourself see it because you want to be a relativist.

Libby: We're getting nowhere except into insults again. Are we finished for tonight?

'Isa: Yes. Tonight can be short. Tomorrow we have many arguments to explore.

Interview 5

The Argument for Relativism from Self-Esteem and from Cultural Relativity

Libby: You should be looking forward to this interview, Professor.

'Isa: Why?

Libby: Because I know you love argument as a little kid loves ice cream. And after all our preliminaries, finally we get to the arguments today.

'Isa: It's only the arguments for relativism today. The arguments for absolutism come later.

Libby: And there's another reason to look forward to today: We agreed to exchange places today. You'll be the interviewer, and I'll be the philosopher—the philosopher defending relativism.

'Isa: Yes, that was our plan.

Libby: Because a relativist should do a better job presenting the arguments for relativism than an absolutist would do. A fairer job, anyway, even if she's not a professional philosopher.

'Isa: Agreed. So how many arguments for relativism have you come up with?

Libby: Eight. And you're going to have to refute every one of them, because if any one remains standing, I've won—I mean relativism has won. Right?

'Isa: That's right.

Libby: Now all we do today is that I just *explain* the arguments for relativism, right? You get to try to answer them next time.

'Isa: That's the plan. So here's my first question.

Libby: But I didn't give you any of my arguments yet. I didn't say anything yet. What are you questioning already?

'Isa: Before we get to each of your eight arguments, one by one, I have a question about what you're doing.

Libby: I'm arguing for relativism.

'Isa: Yes, but why? Are you just doing that to please me . . .

Libby: Fat chance!

'Isa: Or to please our host? Or to play a little game? Our price for a week at the beach?

Libby: It's a great beach, and a small price, but—I really believe in the philosophy I'm defending, if that's what you mean.

'Isa: And do you also believe in arguing for what you believe?

Libby: You know I do.

'Isa: So you believe that good rational arguments can really prove things to be true?

Libby: What things?

'Isa: Do you think relativism can be proved by logical argument?

Libby: That's what I'm doing today, isn't it?

'Isa: Proving it to be true?

Libby: Of course.

'Isa: Really true?

Libby: Yeah, really true. *You're* going to have to try to prove it false.

'Isa: So that means you believe in objective truth, even though you don't believe in objective goodness, right?

Libby: What do you mean by that?

'Isa: You believe in objective truth, because you're going to try to prove relativism is really true. And you don't believe in objective goodness, because that's what relativism means: "There is nothing good or bad but thinking makes it so."

Libby: Yeah, I guess so. Are you going to argue about *that* now? Oh, I think I get it: you're going to try to stop me before I start by saying I'm contradicting myself in arguing for relativism at all because there's a contradiction in believing in objective truth but not objective goodness. Is that your next line?

'Isa: No, I just wanted to know where you stand, what your assumptions are. Because if you didn't believe in objective truth, arguments would be just toys, or games, or jokes. Or misleading ways of expressing personal feelings. But you want your arguments to be taken seriously. You think they can prove their conclusion is *true*.

Libby: That conclusion being relativism. Yes.

'Isa: Fine. I just wanted to know if you took all this reasoning seriously. What's your first argument, then?

Libby: That moral absolutism has three really bad consequences for real live persons, however logical it might be. It makes you unhappy, unfree, and guilty. If you believe in an absolute moral law, you're miserable. Absolutism is unloving and uncaring and inhuman and impersonal and unfeeling and uncompassionate.

'Isa: Wow! All those nasty names! Could you put that argument into a syllogism instead of a list of nasty names?

Libby: Why, sure! I'm a darn sight more logical than you give me credit for, Professor. How's this?—Good morality has good consequences, and bad morality has bad consequences. Happiness and freedom and self-esteem are good consequences, and unhappiness and unfreedom and guilt are bad consequences. Absolutism gives you those bad consequences, and relativism gives you the good consequences. Therefore absolutism is bad, and relativism is good. How's that for logic?

'Isa: Very good. You've given a *moral* reason for rejecting traditional morality.

Libby: I'm not sure whether I'm being insulted or complimented. Do you mean that's a self-contradiction? Are you trying to refute my arguments already?

'Isa: No, we agreed to wait till next time for that. So I won't say anything about it yet. Shall we go on to your second argument, then?

Libby: No. This is too easy on you. All you have to do is ask, "First argument, please." "Second argument, please." "Third argument, please."

'Isa: I agree. It's too easy. It feels unnatural to just let the argument sit up there and not do anything to it. I want to evaluate it once I see it.

Libby: Sure, that's because you're totally judgmental. But *I* want to change our format too, for a different reason. I think it would be better to evaluate each argument as it's presented, instead of waiting till all eight are out there—did I say I had eight?—because we'd just have to repeat each one before evaluating it, next time; and that's a waste of time and tape. We won't remember all eight unless we repeat them. My memory isn't that good. I don't know about yours.

'Isa: It's much worse than yours, I'm sure. You never hear of an "absent minded journalist", do you? Just the "absent minded professor". OK, so we change our schedule—if that's all right with our gracious host.

Kreeft: Of course. Do what you think will work best. I trust your judgment, both of you.

'Isa: Goody! That means I get to chew on your argument right now, Libby.

Libby: Chew away, Professor. But watch out you don't break your teeth. It's a strong argument.

'Isa: Do you think it's your strongest?

Libby: Probably. That's why I put it first. It's the people reason, the popular reason, the reason most people are relativists.

'Isa: Because absolutism makes them feel guilty. [

Libby: Yes. And relativism doesn't.

'Isa: I think we should begin by clarifying a term: the word *because*. When we say "people believe in relativism because . . ." the word *because* is ambiguous. So I have to know how you mean it before I evaluate it. *Because* can mean a subjective, psychological *motive*, something that pushes us from inside, so to speak; or it can mean an objective, logical *reason*, something that pulls us from outside. Do you see the difference? "I believe you *because* I feel like it" versus "I believe you *because* of the evidence, because your premises prove your conclusion".

Libby: So you want to know which *because* it is? It's both.

'**Isa:** Then I will admit that you are right in one sense, but not the other. I agree with you that people abandon moral absolutism *because* it makes them feel guilty. I think the fear of guilt may be a very powerful *motive* for not believing in moral absolutism. But I don't think it's a good *reason*, a good argument.

Libby: Wait—before you get into the logic of the argument—I don't think you can just dismiss the psychological thing like that. If something makes you unhappy, that's a legitimate reason for avoiding it. Especially if it makes *other* people unhappy. I don't want anyone I love to be unhappy. So I hate absolutism because I love people and I don't like to see them suffer. That may not be good logic, but I think it's good psychology.

'**Isa:** Then let's examine the psychology. You reject absolutism because it makes other people unhappy. Right?

Libby: Right.

'**Isa:** I think that's bad logic *and* bad psychology. Bad logic because your conclusion does not follow from your premise. You say it can't be good simply because it makes someone unhappy. And bad psychology because your premise isn't even true psychologically. I don't think an absolute moral law *does* make people unhappy or unfree. I think it makes them happier and freer. And so it's the loving thing. It's like a true, clear label on a bottle of poison, or a road map, or a guard rail on a dangerous road. You're hardly happy if you drink poison or drive off a cliff. You're not free either.

Libby: You mean it's good to sacrifice short-run happiness for greater happiness in the long run.

'**Isa:** Yes.

Libby: Not if it's not *necessary*. Maybe we can be happy both now and tomorrow. So we don't have to sacrifice happiness today for happiness tomorrow.

'Isa: What if your conscience is going to bother you tomorrow?

Libby: Oh, you mean guilt. Yes, let's talk about guilt. Relativism cures that terrible disease. Do you have any idea of all the harm and all the unhappiness and all the misery that all the guilt in the world has caused all the people in the world?

'Isa: I think I do. But I don't think *you* have any idea of the *greater* unhappiness there is in the long run if there *isn't* any guilt. Guilt obviously makes you unhappy in the short run—like pain. But it's necessary, like physical pain, to avoid greater unhappiness in the long run. You know, there's a disease—I don't know the name of it— where you can't feel any pain at all. All the pain nerves shut down. People with this disease don't usually live very long. Because pain is a warning signal. And so is guilt. Guilt is to the soul what pain is to the body.

Libby: No it isn't. Pain is necessary, I grant you. But guilt isn't.

'Isa: Never?

Libby: Never! If you're happy and you feel good about yourself, and you have no guilt, you're going to behave well and make other people happy, without guilt. If you have a load of guilt, you're going to be miserable and you're going to make others miserable too, you're going to behave badly. Guilt is bad, not good. It's like paranoia, not like pain.

'Isa: Even if that were true—and I don't agree it is—your argument begs the question: you're assuming the relativism you're supposed to be proving. *If* relativism is right and there's no real absolute moral law, then you're right: guilt is as pointless as paranoia. But if there *is* a real moral law, then guilt is realistic, and as practical and as proper as pain, and it's there for the same reason as pain: to prevent real harm. It's like a prophet. We're arguing about whether it's a false prophet or a true prophet. You're assuming that it's a false prophet, that it doesn't tell you the truth about objective reality and the real moral law and where you stand in relation to it. Well, I'm assuming the opposite. You haven't proved my assumption is wrong yet.

Libby: Any psychologist can show you the pathological consequences of guilt.

'**Isa:** Of *pathological* guilt, sure. I'm not defending all guilt, any more than I'm defending all pain. Guilt that just sits there and stews and makes you despair is obviously not good. But guilt that makes you move and change and repent and improve—that's great! That guilt is necessary—*if* there's a real objective standard and we violate it. Guilt tells us the truth—that we've violated the standard—and it moves us away from violating it again. You *want* a bad man to feel guilt, don't you? Do you want Hitler to feel good about himself? If your argument is right, it logically follows that a rapist or a tyrant who feels self-esteem and happiness is better than one who feels guilt.

Libby: That's absurd.

'**Isa:** Yes. And here's how the absurdity came about. Your mistake was an equivocation: you used *better* in two different senses: psychologically and morally better. The rapist who feels good about himself is *happier* than the one who feels guilt, but he's not *morally* better. Just psychologically better, more well adjusted. Well adjusted to evil!

Libby: But absolutism produces *morally* bad feelings too: self-righteousness.

'**Isa:** Now I think you're contradicting yourself.

Libby: How's that, Logic Man?

'**Isa:** You've got a self-contradiction within the list of feelings you're taking as moral indicators. You put *guilt* and *self-righteousnss* together as bad feelings and bad moral indicators, right? They both come from absolutism, and they're both bad, right?

Libby: Right . . .

'**Isa:** But they're opposites. Self-righteousness is precisely the *absence* of guilt.

Libby: Hmm . . .

'**Isa:** Perhaps there's more than just a logical self-contradiction here. Perhaps there's a personal self-contradiction.

Libby: What do you mean?

'**Isa:** I mean it's really the relativist who's defending self-righteousness, in defending guiltlessness. Yet the relativist is accusing the *absolutist* of self-righteousness!

Libby: Are you getting personal again?

'Isa: No, I'm getting logical. Let's both try to stick to the issue.

Libby: I still say both those bad feelings come from absolutism.

'Isa: Let's let that go. There's a bigger logical error in your argument. You're begging the question. Even if those bad feelings do come from absolutism, if you're arguing that absolutism has to be rejected for that reason, you're begging the question because you're assuming that feelings are the standard for judging morality.

Libby: Where?

'Isa: In your premise that good morality is one that produces good feelings, and bad morality is one that causes bad feelings. But the claim of absolutism is exactly the opposite: that morality is the standard for judging feelings, not feelings the standard for judging morality. So you're begging the question again: you're assuming the relativism you're supposed to be proving.

Libby: Hmm! Maybe so, maybe not. Your logic confuses me. But reality doesn't. So let's go on to the second argument, because that's based on reality, on simple fact.

'Isa: I'm just the opposite: logic doesn't confuse me; reality often does. I find it very mysterious. Don't you?

Libby: Don't go get personal, now, Professor. Just listen to my argument. It's based on a simple scientific fact.

'Isa: Oh? What fact? What science?

Libby: The facts discovered by anthropologists and sociologists. Moral relativism is simply a historical fact. Different cultures and societies have very different moral values. Different individuals too. Only very provincial people blind themselves to that fact. That's just data. You talk about your argument from data? Well, here's my data. For instance, in Eskimo culture, euthanasia is good; it's right. When you get very old, they put you out on an ice floe so that the rest of the family can survive on the little food that's left. In Christian America, that would be wrong, it would be murder.

'Isa: Pre-Kevorkian America, you mean.

Libby: Yeah. And sex was once taboo everywhere outside the marriage bed, when people were narrow and provincial. Now, it's everybody's right.

'Isa: Ah, yes. The romanticization of fornication.

Libby: Say *what?*

'Isa: The ro . . .

Libby: I heard you. I just haven't heard old-fogey provincialisms like that for many years.

'Isa: I wonder who's being provincial here: the MTV teenie-bopper who's never even heard the word *chastity* except as a funny personal name or the old fogey who lives it.

Libby: I won't be put off by your rhetoric, Professor. The facts are on my side in this one. Anybody who thinks values aren't relative to cultures is just ignorant of facts.

'Isa: The facts of cultural diversity?

Libby: Yeah. Even philosophers should know their facts. And the fact is, as Descartes said, in his *Discourse on Method*, there's no idea so strange that some philosopher hasn't seriously believed it. And there's no deed so strange that some society hasn't legitimized it—cannibalism, for instance, or genocide. And no deed so legitimate that some society hasn't illegitimized it—like entering a temple without a hat on. Or in other societies, *with* a hat on. It's all relative to the culture.

'Isa: Period. Case closed.

Libby: That's right.

'Isa: Let's see if that's right, all right? Let's do a little logic lesson.

Libby: Here comes the dance! Let's see how the philosopher dances away from the facts this time.

'Isa: I don't dance. I just judge your argument on its logical merits.

Libby: Here come de judge!

'Isa: Yes, but the judge is not me but the laws of logic.

Libby: Look, world! Behold the laws of logic incarnate, in Professor Ben Adam!

'Isa: If we could please get down to business, let's look at the structure of your argument.

Libby: You people are so serious!

'Isa: I won't bite that bait, Libby. I'll bite only on your argument today, not your rhetoric. Here—look—to get any moral conclusion, to have any moral argument, you need two premises: a major premise about values and a minor premise about facts. "Murder is wrong; genocide is murder; therefore genocide is wrong." "Charity is good; welfare is charity; therefore welfare is good." Do you see the structure?

Libby: Yes . . .

'Isa: So you can't just say, "Here's the fact; case closed." You can't get a conclusion about values from one premise alone, from the factual premise alone. If there's no value term in the premises, you can't logically get one in the conclusion. That's a non sequitur.

Libby: A what?

'Isa: Latin for "it does not follow". It's a fallacy. The fallacy of getting more out of less, or something out of nothing. Like pulling a rabbit out of an empty hat.

Libby: So I'll just stick in another premise.

'Isa: You've done that already. You've implied a premise, but you haven't stated it. Your argument is an enthymeme.

Libby: A what?

'Isa: An enthymeme. An argument with one premise implied but not stated. *Enthymeme* is Greek for "in the mind". The hidden premise is kept in your mind but not stated.

Libby: How do you know what's in my mind?

'Isa: I don't. But I'll give you the benefit of the doubt. I'll supply your hidden premise for you, and I'll make it the only premise that will make your argument logical, that will prove your conclusion.

Libby: Gee, thanks, Professor. Somehow I suspect your gift is going to be a Trojan horse. (See, I know a little about Greece too!)

'Isa: Here: Your argument was this: moral rightness and wrongness are relative to culture because what's right in one culture is wrong in another—right? Wasn't that your argument?

Libby: Yes.

'Isa: A culture's values differ from one culture to another; therefore moral rightness differs from one culture to another. Right?

Libby: Right.

'Isa: Do you see the hidden assumption of that argument? It's that moral rightness is a matter of obedience to your culture's values, that it's right to obey your culture's values. That's your hidden premise. Only if you combine that premise with the other one can you prove your conclusion. You're assuming that moral rightness is defined by culture, and then you go on and say that cultures differ; therefore moral rightness differs.

Libby: Wait a minute. Let's get that out on the table. Can we put this down on paper where we can see it? I like diagrams . . .

Kreeft: It all has to be on the tape. We all agreed to that, remember? So if you do diagrams, you have to put them on the tape somehow.

Libby: OK, I can do it in my head. No problem.

'Isa: But there *is* a problem. Your argument begs the question.

Libby: Again?

'Isa: Your implied premise *assumes* the cultural relativism you're supposed to be *proving*. You see, the moral absolutist *denies* that it's always right to obey your culture's values. He denies your implied premise. He has a universal standard, a natural law; and by that higher law he can criticize a whole culture's values as wrong. That's why only an absolutist can be a progressive. The relativist can only be a conservative.

Libby: Hey, wait a minute! Now you're dancing backwards. We liberals are always the progressives, and we're the relativists. You conservatives are always the absolutists. You've got it all backwards.

'**Isa:** No, *you* have it backwards. If you're a relativist, that means you think values are relative to cultures, right?

Libby: Yes . . .

'**Isa:** So you have no universal law, no higher law, no higher standard than culture, right?

Libby: Right. We don't claim to have a private telephone line to heaven, like you.

'**Isa:** So you can't criticize your culture, then. Your culture sets the standard. Your culture creates the commandments. Your culture is God. "My country right or wrong." That doesn't sound like progressivism to me. That sounds like status quo conservatism.

Libby: You're confusing me. You make everything stand on its head.

'**Isa:** No, *you* do. Or your media do, and you've been suckered by them. It's a big lie; it's pure propaganda. If you just stop and think for yourself for a minute, you'll see that it's really just the opposite of the media stereotypes. Only a believer in an absolute higher law can criticize a whole culture. He's the rebel, the radical, the prophet who can say to a whole culture, "You're worshipping a false God and a false good. Change!" That's the absolutist; and that's the force for change. The Jews changed history more than anyone because they were absolutists—the conscience for the world, the Jewish mother who makes you feel guilty about not calling her, not calling on God, not praying. Or guilty about vegging out in front of the TV instead of going out and getting an education and getting a job and changing the world.

Libby: Not fair! The relativist is for change too.

'**Isa:** But he has no *moral* basis for it. All a relativist can say to a Hitler is, "Different strokes for different folks, and I like my strokes and I hate yours." The absolutist can say, "You and your whole society are wrong and wicked, and divine justice will destroy you, inescapably, unless you repent." Which of those two messages is more progressive? Which one is the force for change?

Libby: OK, there *is* a problem here: How does a relativist generate moral passion for changing a culture without a natural law above that culture? I guess it's just got to be personal passion, individual conscience.

'Isa: OK, suppose it is conscience. Does conscience *discover* the moral law or *create* it?

Libby: If I say we discover it, you'll say, "*Where* is the law we discover?" And if I answer that it's in the culture, I'm back where I started. But if I say it's in God, or in a higher law, I'm not a relativist any more.

'Isa: Now you're suddenly becoming very logical.

Libby: So I have to say we create it; we don't discover it. It's subjective, not objective. And we create the passion for it because it's ours, like a work of art.

'Isa: But then there's no moral justification for it. It's just the rules of the game you created. It's not *right*; it's just *yours*. What justifies you in creating one set of laws instead of another? You're back in Mussolini's relativism then. Remember that quote? From the first interview?

Libby: Remember it? I'm haunted by it. Honestly, that connection really bothers me. But I can't just give up relativism, because I can't dispute the facts, and the facts still show that different cultures have different values.

'Isa: No, I don't think so. I think you're confused about your "facts". And that's a second weakness in your cultural relativism argument: in your supposedly factual premise that different cultures have different values, there's an equivocation, an ambiguity in that term *values*. Remember our little history lesson the other day. That term *values* was *never* used in ethics until quite recently. You know why? Because it's inherently ambiguous. The modern relativist takes advantage of that ambiguity. The ambiguity is between *subjective opinions* about morality —about good, or right, or ought—versus *objective truth* about what's really good or right or obligatory.

Libby: Wait a minute. Your distinction doesn't make any sense to me. "Objective truth about values"—that's meaningless. You can't have objective truth about *values*. They're not facts, not data. You can't see them. They're how you *feel about* what you see. Like colored glasses that you look through to see black and white stuff—the color comes from you.

'Isa: But that's the whole issue. That's the conclusion again. You can't assume it as your premise without begging the question again.

Libby: But you're assuming just as much as I am. You're assuming you *can* have objective truth about values. It's just my assumption against yours. You haven't shown me that you *can* have objective truth about things you can't see.

'Isa: Then let me do just that right now. OK?

Libby: How are you going to do that?

'Isa: Just by asking you a few questions.

Libby: Oh, right, Socrates. I'm onto your trick. Once I answer one question your way, you pounce. One false move, and you're five moves ahead checkmating me. Just because you're better at that game than I am, doesn't mean . . .

'Isa: No, no, all you have to do is be honest. Just answer what you really think. Is that so hard?

Libby: OK, let's try it. But, you know, you're getting farther and farther from an *interview*.

'Isa: Let's call it a Socratic interview.

Libby: Oh, right! I don't think any of those poor victims of Socrates thought he was just an *interviewer*. But go ahead. I'm a glutton for punishment.

'Isa: Do you believe God exists?

Libby: Yeah, but not the way you do.

'Isa: But you believe he's real.

Libby: No, I believe *she's* real. Like I said, "not the way you do".

'Isa: That doesn't matter for now. So you're not an atheist.

Libby: No.

'Isa: An atheist believes there's no God. You believe there's some God, some kind of God.

Libby: Right.

'Isa: Can you see God with your senses?

Libby: Of course not.

'Isa: But if you're right, he's there anyway—oops, sorry, I mean *God* is there anyway, right?

Libby: It's OK, you can use your male chauvinist language if you like. I know it's a great comfort for you. Yeah, I believe God is really there. She's there for me, but not for the atheist.

'Isa: And when you die, you expect to meet him, right?

Libby: I guess so.

'Isa: And then you'll *know* he's real, instead of just *believing* it, right?

Libby: OK.

'Isa: And if the atheist dies, he might meet God too, if he's really there, right?

Libby: I don't know. How should I know?

'Isa: But he *might* meet God, if God is real. He won't meet an elf if elves aren't real, right? Do you believe elves are real?

Libby: No . . .

'Isa: Then the atheist won't meet a real elf after he dies, because there are no real elves. Right?

Libby: Right.

'Isa: But he might meet God, if there is a God, if your belief is right and the atheist's belief is wrong.

Libby: And if I say yes to that?

'Isa: Then you just distinguished subjective opinions about God, or beliefs about God, from the objective truth about God. One of those two opinions—yours or the atheist's—is wrong, because it's not the same as the objective truth.

Libby: Maybe the *atheist's* belief is true. Maybe *I'll* be the one who's surprised when I die. I don't *know* that, I just *believe*.

'Isa: Yes, but you distinguished *belief* from *truth*. One of the two beliefs—yours or the atheist's—is not true, and the other is. Because either there is no God at all, or there is some kind of God.

Libby: OK.

'Isa: But you can't see God.

Libby: Right.

'Isa: So you just admitted making a distinction between subjective opinion and objective truth about something you couldn't see: God.

Libby: I guess I did—about God, anyway.

'Isa: A minute ago you said you couldn't do that: distinguish subjective opinion from objective truth about something you couldn't see. You said you couldn't have objective truth about the things you can't see, like moral values. I thought you were arguing that moral values aren't visible, and you can't have objective truth about things that aren't visible. Therefore you can't have objective truth about moral values. Didn't you say something like that?

Libby: And I still say that. I don't claim I have the objective truth about God. I just believe in her.

'Isa: But you believe that your belief is *true*, don't you? You believe God is really *real*. That's what you said. I know you don't think you can *prove* God, or even be *certain* that God is real, but you do *believe* that God is real, don't you?—really, truly, objectively there—so real that even an atheist might meet God and find out that his belief, his atheism, was wrong.

Libby: Yeah, I guess I believe that.

'Isa: Then there can be objective truth about invisible things.

Libby: Maybe only about God.

'Isa: What about life after death? You can't see that now, can you?

Libby: No.

'Isa: But it's either real or not. Either you'll still be conscious after your body dies, or not. So *somebody* knows the objective truth about life after death: either the believer or the unbeliever.

Libby: But nobody can prove it. Nobody can be certain.

'Isa: Maybe not. But *somebody's* belief is in fact objectively true, even if they can't be certain which one.

Libby: Yeah, that's right.

'Isa: And what about happiness, or love, or beauty, or even numbers? None of them have size and shape and color; none of them can be perceived by the body's five senses. Yet there's objective truth about them. One person can be right, and another person can be wrong about them.

Libby: But nobody can know who's wrong about love or beauty . . .

'Isa: Maybe, maybe not. You can certainly know who's wrong in mathematics.

Libby: That's because you can *prove* it in math. You can't prove it in . . . you can't prove the other stuff.

'Isa: I think you can. But even if you can't, you can sometimes *know* even when you can't *prove*. For instance, happiness. Suppose I believe you're happy. I can't *see* happiness. I *believe* it's in your soul now. Then you suddenly say something nasty and I realize I was wrong: you were really unhappy, not happy.

Libby: That's only because you heard me say something. You sensed it, with your ears.

'Isa: But the *happiness* isn't sensed with the ears or any other physical sense. What I sensed was a visible *effect* of invisible happiness. Like sensing the universe as a visible effect of the invisible God.

Libby: You get me confused with your abstractions.

'Isa: Then let's try to sort them out. Let's distinguish five simple questions. One: Is it objectively *real* or not? Two: If it *is* real, do I *know* it's real, or not? Three: If I can know it, is that knowledge *certain* or is it only probable, or faith, or right opinion? Four: If it's certain, can I *prove* it to others, can I make them certain too by logical argument, or is it only a private certainty that I can't share? And five: If I *can* prove it, is this proof a strict *scientific method* proof or not?

Libby: I guess I can understand those distinctions . . .

'**Isa:** Let's be sure. First one: If a thing can't be known, do you think it can't be real? Or do you think there might be something real that we can't know? Is "the unknown" a possible category?

Libby: Of course there might be something real that we can't know.

'**Isa:** OK. Next one: Is all knowledge certain? If you know something, do you think you must know it with certainty? Or is "true opinion" or "probable knowledge" a possible category?

Libby: It is.

'**Isa:** OK. Third: Is all certainty provable? If you're certain of something—for instance, that you are really happy now—might you be unable to prove it to someone else?

Libby: Of course.

'**Isa:** OK, now one more: Is there any other kind of proof than the scientific method?

Libby: That I have my doubts about.

'**Isa:** When was the scientific method discovered and used?

Libby: I don't know—some time around the Renaissance, I think.

'**Isa:** In modern times, anyway.

Libby: Yeah.

'**Isa:** Well, didn't anyone ever prove anything at all with a good, certain, logical proof before that? Were *none* of the arguments of the Greek philosophers logical proofs?

Libby: OK, maybe some were, maybe there are some good proofs that aren't purely scientific. So what? How does this relate to moral absolutism? We seem to have gotten off into a logic lesson.

'**Isa:** I was trying to show you how you equivocated on the term *values* in your cultural relativism argument.

Libby: Oh, my poor saintly grandmother! She'd turn over in her grave. Her granddaughter, an equivocator! She wanted me to be a doctor. Do you think I'm going to jail? I'll bet the Puritans would have put me in the stocks. What's the punishment today for equivocating in public in Massachusetts?

'Isa: The punishment is losing the argument—and being forced to understand where you made your mistake. You equivocated between value-*opinions* and *values*, between *opinions* about what's right or wrong and what's *really* right or wrong. You see, different cultures may have different *opinions* about what's morally right and wrong, just as they have different opinions about what happens after death; but that doesn't prove your conclusion that what's right in one culture is wrong in another. What's *believed* to be right and what really *is* right aren't necessarily the same, just as what's believed to exist after death and what really exists aren't necessarily the same. We can be wrong about it. Just because I may believe there is no hell doesn't mean there is none or that I won't go there. If it did, the infallible way to be saved would be just stop believing in hell! You see? Just because a good Nazi *thinks* that genocide is right, that's doesn't mean it is.

Libby: Unless "there is nothing good or bad but thinking makes it so".

'Isa: But that's the relativist's *conclusion*. It can't also be your premise, without begging the question, assuming what you have to prove.

Libby: But it might still be true. Maybe values *are* nothing but beliefs. I mean *opinions*. "Beliefs" sounds too religious. Let's call values "opinions".

'Isa: Well, then, since you reduce values to opinions, we need to examine the meaning of "opinion". An opinion is always an opinion *about* something, right?

Libby: I guess so.

'Isa: The technical word philosophers use is *intentional*. An opinion *intends* something; it points to something, like a sign. It refers to something; it has a referent.

Libby: OK, so what?

'Isa: So there are two kinds of opinions: right opinions and wrong opinions. Right opinions match their referent; wrong opinions don't.

Libby: OK. So?

'Isa: So if values are only opinions, what is their referent? What are they opinions *about*?

Libby: About right and wrong.

'Isa: And is right and wrong a *fact* or an *opinion*?

Libby: An opinion.

'Isa: So values are only opinions, and these opinions are opinions about right and wrong—which are only opinions. So values are opinions about opinions. You see where this leads you? Infinite regress: opinions about opinions about opinions about opinions, with no *referent*. There's nothing for all these opinions to opine! It's like a hall of mirrors with nothing in them to reflect.

Libby: OK, so they're opinions about *facts*, then. But only *opinions* about facts, not facts. *Facts* are things you can *see*.

'Isa: But that just doesn't square with how we use language. "Thou shalt not murder" clearly isn't an opinion about facts, about whether there will be a murder or not. "Courage is good" isn't an opinion about how many people are in fact courageous.

Libby: That's true. So what?

'Isa: So values can't be either opinions about opinions or opinions about facts. So values can't be mere opinions.

Libby: Even so, they're still relative to cultures, whatever they are.

'Isa: Because different cultures have different values?

Libby: Yeah, that's the hard fact. You can't argue that away. You got your logic, but I got my facts.

'Isa: But you don't! Your "argument from facts" doesn't even have its facts right! Cultures *don't* differ totally about values, even if you mean only value *opinions* or beliefs. There's a massive agreement about values.

Libby: Oh yeah? What cave have you been in, Professor? Haven't you ever taken a course in anthropology? Or even philosophy—what about Nietzsche's "transvaluation of all values"?

'Isa: That was his own insane little private dream. No culture ever existed that believed and taught what Nietzsche called for.

Libby: But there have been tremendous differences about values.

'**Isa:** Yes, but never total. There's always some deeper underlying agreement beneath every disagreement. It's like when you visit a strange country: you experience an initial shock because the language is so different; but then, beneath the different *words*, you find the same *concepts*. That's what makes translation possible.

Libby: But that's language, not morality.

'**Isa:** It's analogous. Beneath different cultural customs and laws you find common values, similar *morals* beneath different *mores*.

Libby: I don't think you do.

'**Isa:** Sure you do. The moral agreement among Moses and Buddha and Jesus and Muhammad and Confucius and Lao Tzu and Socrates and Solomon and Cicero and Zoroaster and Hammurabi—that's massive. That's far greater than their differences.

Libby: I don't know about that.

'**Isa:** That's because you've studied ideology instead of science in those anthropology classes.

Libby: Look, maybe there are some important similarities, but there are a lot more differences, and if you don't know *that*, then *you're* the one who didn't study science.

'**Isa:** Sure there are differences—a lot of little differences circling around a big agreement, like fleas around an elephant. Your teachers just ignore the elephant.

Libby: The differences are bigger than fleas!

'**Isa:** OK, the image was an exaggeration; but the differences are usually differences in emphasis, not a whole new value system. For instance, most premodern societies valued courage more than compassion, while most modern societies value compassion more than courage. But neither society says cowardice is good, and neither one says cruelty is good. There's never been the wholesale relativism of opinion about values that the relativists teach as history. It's false history. It's a lie!

Libby: So you think all the moral disagreements in history are just matters of degree?

'**Isa:** Either that, or else they're disagreements about how to apply a more basic value they both agree on. I think you can always find that in moral arguments: whenever there's disagreement about one value, there's always agreement on a more basic level about a more basic value.

Libby: Where's the agreement between the Nazis and the democracies? Genocide sounds pretty basic to me!

'**Isa:** Why did the Nazis want genocide? They claimed it improved humanity. They believed Aryan racial superiority was good for the world, that it would make a perfect world. Both sides wanted to improve humanity; they differed on *how.*

Libby: And you say that the Nazis were good, sincere people, just a little confused?

'**Isa:** Of course not . . .

Libby: But are you saying the difference was minor?

'**Isa:** No. I'm saying that beneath a moral difference you always find some more basic moral agreement. Otherwise it's not a *moral* argument at all. Because all argument needs a common premise. Moral disagreements between cultures are just like moral disagreements between individuals that way: unless there's some common premise, you can't have disagreement about how to apply that premise.

Libby: But those disagreements can be terribly important!

'**Isa:** Yes, but never total. You can't even *imagine* a totally new morality, any more than you can imagine a totally new universe, or set of numbers, or colors. Just try. Try to imagine a society where honesty and justice and courage and self-control and faith and hope and charity are *evil,* and lying and cheating and stealing and cowardice and betrayal and addiction and despair and hate are all *good.* You just can't do it.

Libby: Didn't Milton have a line for that? "Evil, be thou my good!"

'**Isa:** Yes, that was Satan's line, in *Paradise Lost.* The society we're trying to imagine does exist after all—in hell.

Libby: Oops.

'**Isa:** And maybe in a few of hell's colonies on earth. I grant you that societies can go off the tracks very badly, just as individuals can. But that doesn't prove relativism. In fact, it presupposes absolutism, because absolutism means the tracks are really there, transcending societies and judging the bad society.

Libby: Look. The tape's almost ended. Let's quit for this morning and do the other questions later. It's getting too hot for any place but the beach.

'**Isa:** Sorry if I turned up the heat.

Libby: Don't flatter yourself. The heat out there, I mean. God turned that up, not you.

'**Isa:** Maybe he turned up the other heat too, not me. I didn't invent the laws of logic, you know.

Libby: Oooh, wow! Late-breaking news item! Professor Ben Adam did *not* invent the laws of logic, despite all appearances. I guess that has to be it for this morning.

'**Isa:** Just because the tape's used up? Can't we do another one if we want, on another tape?

Kreeft: Of course, if you both want to.

Libby: I'm game. But let's have lunch first, and do it this afternoon.

'**Isa:** OK. There's no surf today anyway.

Interview 6

The Arguments for Relativism from
Social Conditioning, Freedom, and Tolerance

Libby: Do you want to go faster this afternoon? I'm not sure how many more interviews we're going to need to cover all eight arguments.

'Isa: *I* don't want to rush. I want to do justice to each one. Don't you?

Libby: Oh, I doubt we'll do that. But I don't want to rush either.

Kreeft: It's OK. Take your time. It doesn't have to be ten interviews. It can be as many as you like—if you can stay longer. You're as welcome as the sun.

'Isa: Thank you. Well, Libby, we are up to your third argument, I think.

Libby: Yes. This one is based on a fact too, a scientifically verifiable fact: the fact that society conditions values in us. If we had been brought up in a Hindu society, we'd all have Hindu values.

'Isa: And what does that prove?

Libby: That the origin of values is human minds—parents and teachers—rather than something objective to human minds. And what comes from human subjects is subjective, so values are subjective —like the rules of a game—although they can be public and agreed to by the whole community, like the rules of baseball. They look absolute because they're universally agreed on. But that's just because they came from consensus. They're relative to the people who made them. They have creators. They're not eternal.

'Isa: This third argument of yours seems very similar to the second one.

Libby: Because both are based on facts.

'Isa: No, because both confuse values with value-opinions.

Libby: Somehow I thought you'd say that.

'Isa: Perhaps society conditions value-opinions in us, as you say. But that doesn't mean society conditions values in us, unless values are nothing but value-opinions. But that's precisely the point at issue, the conclusion. It can't also be the premise without begging the question again.

Libby: That was short and sweet.

'Isa: You also have a false assumption in your argument.

Libby: Where?

'Isa: The argument says that values are conditioned in us by society; therefore they're subjective. That logically assumes that whatever is conditioned in us by society is subjective. Right?

Libby: Yeah, that's the logic. But what's wrong with that assumption?

'Isa: It's just not true. We learn the rules of baseball from society, and they're subjective; but we also learn the rules of physics and mathematics from society, and they're *not* subjective, not man-made.

Libby: Who do you think writes the math and physics books? Angels?

'Isa: We make the books, and the language systems, but not the truth.

Libby: How do you know that? Maybe the mind makes it all.

'Isa: Just look at the difference. Our mind creates the rules of baseball. They're not *there* until we make them. And we can change them. But our mind *discovers* the rules of math and physics. And we can't change them.

Libby: OK, so what?

'Isa: So the fact that we learn something from our society doesn't prove that it's subjective.

Libby: Hmm . . .

'**Isa:** And that was your premise, and it's not true. So your argument is worthless.

Libby: May I sulk now?

'**Isa:** No, I'm not finished yet. Your other premise is false too, the one you stated as well as the one you implied. "All values are conditioned in us by society"—that's not true.

Libby: Prove it.

'**Isa:** Gladly. If it were true—if all values were conditioned in us by society—there could be no nonconformity to society. The existence of nonconformists proves the presence of some origin of values that transcends society.

Libby: Maybe the nonconformists just create their own values that are different from society's values. That's why they're nonconformists!

'**Isa:** But then there can't be moral argument between the society and the nonconformists. There can't be moral conflict, only physical conflict, if the two sides have no common morality at all to appeal to. Look at history. Look at facts. Look at actual situations where you have nonconformists, like Socrates or Jesus or Muhammad: they criticize their society by holding it up to a higher moral standard. They don't just fight with physical force; they fight with moral force. They don't say, "In my own name I rebel", but "In the name of justice I rebel."

Libby: Sometimes they do. Everybody knows that. But that doesn't prove anything.

'**Isa:** It's a fact your argument can't explain. You say society conditions all our value-opinions in us. But what about the value-opinions of the nonconformist? *They* didn't get their value-opinions by social conditioning, because they disagree with their social conditioning. A society wouldn't condition someone to rebel against it. It *couldn't*; that would be society conditioning someone not to be conditioned by society.

Libby: I gotta take that one home and think about it. Let's try my fourth argument.

'**Isa:** Be my guest.

Libby: Absolutism says we discover values, and relativism says we create them, right?

'Isa: Right.

Libby: And when we create something, we're creative. It's a free act. You're free to invent baseball. You're not free to change two plus two equals four. Right?

'Isa: Right.

Libby: So relativism gives you freedom, and absolutism takes it away.

'Isa: Is that your argument?

Libby: Yes, and it's our Supreme Court's argument too, in the *Casey* decision. They declared that each individual has a "fundamental right . . . to define the meaning of existence". That's just about the most fundamental right and the most fundamental freedom I can imagine.

'Isa: Yes, that's what they all say in hell.

Libby: What? What? What did I hear you say?

'Isa: Nothing. Forget it. I'll stick to logical analysis. You're arguing that we're not really free if we can't create our own values, is that it?

Libby: That's it.

'Isa: And everybody loves freedom, of course.

Libby: Everybody who's anybody. Everybody who's sane. Sometimes I'm not too sure about people like you.

'Isa: That's the phrase *I* got in trouble with two days ago, remember? No, no, I mustn't do that; I promised I'd stick to logical analysis. OK, look here, freedom can't possibly *create* values, as you say, because freedom *presupposes* values.

Libby: Why does freedom have to presuppose values?

'Isa: Because your argument that relativism is good because it guarantees freedom presupposes that freedom is really valuable, or really good.

Libby: Well, maybe I have to presuppose just that one value, and from that comes all the others. I don't have to presuppose anything else, like your repressive moral laws, and sin, and evil, and all that unfree stuff.

'**Isa:** But if freedom is really good, it must be freedom from something really bad, so you're assuming a real, objective bad as well as a real, objective good.

Libby: Well, just two values then: the value of freedom and the anti-value of unfreedom.

'**Isa:** Freedom for yourself alone, or for everyone?

Libby: For everyone, of course.

'**Isa:** Then you also have to presuppose the value of the Golden Rule, or justice, or equality, or fairness.

Libby: OK, so it's up to three.

'**Isa:** But the third one is the problem. You demand the right to be free to create your own values, right?

Libby: Yes.

'**Isa:** And you grant that right to everybody, right?

Libby: Right.

'**Isa:** Even me?

Libby: Oh, ye gods and goddesses, behold how far my justice and charity extend! Even to him. Yes, Professor, even to you.

'**Isa:** Then I claim that right. And the value system I freely choose to create is one where your opinions have no weight at all, because you are a woman.

Libby: Are you . . . are you serious?

'**Isa:** No, but suppose I were. What could you say? Or suppose I choose to create a value system in which I am God and rightly demand total obedience from you, who are not God. Is that OK with you?

Libby: You're halfway there already, and even *that's* not OK with me. No, it's not OK.

'**Isa:** Because it's insane, it's not true.

Libby: That's for sure.

'Isa: And it's not fair.

Libby: No.

'Isa: So you're presupposing two values: truth, or honesty, or sanity, or realism; and justice, or fairness, or equality.

Libby: No. Those are *my* values, all right; but I'm not claiming they're absolute or universal or objective, just mine.

'Isa: But then your protest against my megalomania and unfairness is no *better* than my protest against your truth and fairness. If you don't appeal to any higher moral value to condemn me, all you can appeal to is your feelings. Or your fists. Emotional force or physical force. And that's hardly a recipe for freedom!

Libby: You and your logic. You can trip up anybody over anything. You just play with words. It doesn't come from experience.

'Isa: Oh, but it does. The simplest refutation of your argument about freedom comes from experience.

Libby: This I gotta see.

'Isa: Yes, you do. We all know from experience that we are free to create different socially acceptable rules for driving and speech and clothing and eating and drinking . . .

Libby: That's just what I'm saying . . .

'Isa: But we also know from experience that we're *not* free to make murder or rape or slavery or treason *right*, or charity and justice *wrong*. We can create different *mores* but not different *morals*. We can no more create a new moral value than a new universe.

Libby: Speak for yourself, little man.

'Isa: You mean some people can do that?

Libby: Maybe. That's what Nietzsche said. Maybe we can all do it if we're only courageous enough.

'Isa: If we could, then what we created wouldn't be moral values at all, just rules of a new game. We wouldn't feel bound by them, or wrong when we disobeyed them, or right when we obeyed them.

Libby: How do you know? You've never tried it.

'Isa: Look. Suppose we were free to create "thou shalt murder" *or* "thou shalt not murder" as we pleased, just as we're free to create "thou shalt play nine innings" or "thou shalt play six innings" as we please. Then we'd feel no more guilty about murder than about playing six innings.

Libby: I repeat: How do you know? You've never tried it. You can't know from experience.

'Isa: But we *can* know from experience that we are bound by some fundamental moral values, like justice and the Golden Rule.

Libby: No we're not. We're free to disobey them if we want. It happens all the time.

'Isa: Oh, sure. We experience our free will to obey or disobey them. But we also experience our lack of freedom to change them into their opposites—to "creatively" make hate good, or love evil, for instance. Try it! You just can't do it. All you can do is refuse the whole moral order and be wicked; you can't make another moral order. And it's experience that teaches us that. We know from experience that we're free to *choose* to hate, but we're not free to experience a moral *obligation* to hate, only to love.

Libby: Hmm. . . . Some people *did* experience a moral obligation to hate, I think.

'Isa: The Marquis de Sade, and Hitler, and Charles Manson maybe. Is *that* the "freedom" your relativism wants? The freedom to "create your own values"—as Mussolini said?

Libby: And if it is?

'Isa: If it is, you need something more basic than an argument. Something more infantile. Something like a spanking.

Libby: If you didn't have that twinkle in your eye, I'd give *you* a spanking for that boorish remark. But that brings up my next argument—from what you don't have: tolerance. So I don't expect you to sympathize with this argument at all. But relativism is tolerant and absolutism is intolerant, and most Americans prefer tolerance—unlike you and your ilk.

'**Isa:** Ah, it's the ilk now, is it? I believe ilk hunting is illegal in this state. But seriously, let's look at the tolerance argument now.

Libby: Gee, I wonder what's coming next! You know, I wish I had just stuck to our original plan, and got all eight of my arguments out into the light of day for a whole minute or two before I let you zap them with your bug zapper logic. You don't even let them live as long as a mayfly—*they* live just twenty-four hours; mine don't even make twenty-four seconds.

'**Isa:** Are you finished complaining? Can we explore the argument now?

Libby: That's what we're here for.

'**Isa:** First, let's be clear what we mean by "tolerance". It's a quality of *people*. But I think your argument makes it a quality of *ideas*. The idea of relativism is what you think is "tolerant" and absolutism is "intolerant"—isn't that what you said?

Libby: Yes, and I still say it.

'**Isa:** But that's a confusion. *Ideas* can't be tolerant. They can be fuzzy, or ill defined, but that doesn't make them *tolerant*, any more than clarity or exactness makes them intolerant. Look—suppose a carpenter tolerates three-sixteenths of an inch deviation from plumb. He's three times more *tolerant* than a carpenter who tolerates only one-sixteenth of an inch deviation. But he's no less *clear*. Or take teachers: Say one teacher tolerates no dissent at all from his fuzzy and ill-defined views, while another teacher tolerates a lot of dissent from his very clearly defined views. You see? The idea of relativism can't be "tolerant" because *no* idea is "tolerant". *People* are tolerant or intolerant; ideas are *clear or unclear*.

Libby: So? So it's relativists that are tolerant, then.

'**Isa:** OK, so now your argument is that a relativist philosophy makes a tolerant philosopher, and an absolutist philosophy makes an intolerant philosopher.

Libby: That's it exactly. Absolutes are hard and unyielding, and if you're their defender, you make yourself in their image: hard and unyielding.

'Isa: But there's absolutely no need of that at all. You can teach hard, absolute facts in a soft, tolerant way, and you can teach soft, relativistic opinions in a hard, intolerant way.

Libby: You *can*, but you usually *don't*. Let's just say that relativism *fosters* tolerant behavior. Experience backs me up there.

'Isa: Let's see. If relativism fosters tolerant behavior, experience should show a smaller percentage of relativists among those who behave intolerantly than among the population at large—few relativist murderers and many relativist saints. Is this what we find? Isn't the opposite closer to the truth? It's the tolerant, compassionate saints who are the moral absolutists, and the intolerant, hardened criminals who are the moral relativists.

Libby: But look at the history of science. Open-mindedness was the key to progress. Old absolutisms held it back for thousands of years.

'Isa: So you think the history of science shows that absolutism fosters intolerance?

Libby: Certainly. Science has made tremendous progress in modern times because of its tolerance of different and "heretical" views.

'Isa: That's true. But science isn't relativistic. It believes in objective truth. It's not about subjective truths, relative to the scientist.

Libby: Therefore . . . what?

'Isa: Therefore belief in absolute objective truth doesn't necessarily foster intolerance.

Libby: Oh. I guess not, not necessarily.

'Isa: And here's another weakness in your argument. If you examine the meaning of "tolerance", you find it always presupposes some objective morality, some objectively real good and evil. Because we don't tolerate *goods*, only *evils*, in order to prevent worse evils. A patient tolerates nausea, from chemotherapy, to avoid death by cancer. A society tolerates smoking, or alcohol, to preserve freedom, or privacy.

Libby: Hmm . . .

'Isa: And here's another weakness. The argument is a non sequitur. The conclusion doesn't follow. Even if your premise were true, even if belief in moral absolutism did cause intolerance, it doesn't follow that absolutism is *false*. A belief could have bad effects but still be true. The mugger's belief that the cop on the beat is sleeping causes him to be intolerant to his victim; but it doesn't follow that the belief is false, that the cop isn't really asleep.

Libby: All that logic . . .

'**Isa:** But the simplest refutation of your "tolerance" argument is your premise. You assume that tolerance is good—really good, universally good, good for everybody. So you're assuming the very moral absolutism you're trying to refute!

Libby: I'm not doing that. How can I assume something I don't believe?

'**Isa:** Then you must be merely affirming your personal subjective preference for tolerance.

Libby: Right.

'**Isa:** But then you're not making any moral demands or claims on others, any more than if you were affirming your personal subjective preference for yogurt, or your favorite movie star.

Libby: No, tolerance isn't like yogurt. That's a stupid analogy.

'**Isa:** Everyone should have it?

Libby: Yes.

'**Isa:** But not because it's from God, or a higher law, or anything like that.

Libby: Right.

'**Isa:** We made it up, just as we created every other moral value.

Libby: That's what I say.

'**Isa:** It's not *the* truth, it's *your* truth.

Libby: Exactly.

'**Isa:** Then you're demanding everybody live by your truth. Isn't that intolerant?

Libby: Not if everybody else feels the same way.

'Isa: But they don't! Many people and many cultures don't think tolerance is always good. Some think it's a weakness.

Libby: That's true. Many cultures in the past were very insensitive to tolerance.

'Isa: So you have a dilemma when it comes to cross-cultural tolerance. Should you tolerate other cultures' intolerance, or not?

Libby: Suppose I say yes? Tolerate all other cultures.

'Isa: Then you'd better stop bad-mouthing the Spanish Inquisition.

Libby: Hmm. And if I say no? *Don't* tolerate intolerance?

'Isa: *Why* not? *Why* do you say, "Don't tolerate intolerance"?

Libby: Because intolerance stinks. Because the Spanish Inquisition deserves to be bad-mouthed.

'Isa: Then you're appealing to a universal, objective value transcending different cultures.

Libby: No, we just prefer tolerance. It's our consensus.

'Isa: But history's consensus is against it. Why impose ours? Isn't that culturally intolerant?

Libby: I don't know. But I do know that intolerance is regress. We all know that today (with a few exceptions, perhaps, a few dinosaurs to be interviewed). We've progressed far from those bad old days when people like you ruled the world.

'Isa: Ah, but that very notion—of moral progress—presupposes moral absolutism.

Libby: No way.

'Isa: Oh, yes. You can make progress only if there's an objective standard toward which you're progressing. "Progress" doesn't mean just "change", but change for the better. The very idea of progress presupposes a real "better" and a real "good". In fact, an unchanging one.

Libby: What? How do you get that?

'**Isa:** Imagine you're a runner. How could you make progress toward a moving goal line? One that ran away from you as fast as you ran toward it?

Libby: Hmm . . .

'**Isa:** But the main argument, the simplest argument, is just this: if no moral values are absolute, neither is tolerance. The absolutist can take tolerance much more seriously than the relativist. It's absolutism, not relativism, that fosters tolerance. In fact, it's relativism that fosters *intolerance.*

Libby: That's ridiculous.

'**Isa:** No it isn't. Because . . . *why not* be intolerant? Only because it feels better to you? What happens tomorrow when it feels different? *Why* be tolerant? Only because it's our society's consensus? What happens tomorrow, when the consensus changes? You see? The relativist can't appeal to a moral law as a wall, a dam against intolerance. But we need a dam because societies are fickle, like individuals. What else can deter a Germany—a humane and humanistic Germany in the twenties—from turning to an inhumane and inhuman Nazi philosophy in the thirties? What else can stop a now-tolerant America from some future intolerance?—against any group it decides to oppress? It was Blacks in the Southeast over slavery last century; it may be Hispanics in the Southwest over immigration next century. We're intolerant to unwanted unborn babies today; we'll start killing born ones tomorrow. Maybe eventually teenagers. They're sometimes "wanted" even less than babies!

Libby: You're getting more and more ridiculous.

'**Isa:** Then answer the question: *Why not?* That's the question. We persecuted homosexuals yesterday; today we persecute homophobes; maybe tomorrow we'll go back to persecuting homosexuals again. *Why not,* if morals are only relative?

Libby: You're a very dangerous man, you know. I'll bet you're a homophobe too. You absolutists usually are. How right they are to fear you!

'**Isa:** "They"?

Libby: Gays, lesbians, anyone you call "them".

'Isa: You used the pronoun, not me. But they're *not* right to fear us. We're their *defenders*, we absolutists.

Libby: Yeah, right! Sell me the Brooklyn Bridge next, why don't you?

'Isa: No, really . . .

Libby: Why do they all fear you then?

'Isa: Not all. Many do, I grant you. But they shouldn't. Because the same moral absolutism they fear because it's not tolerant of their behavior is their only secure protection against intolerance of their persons. The same morality that says "always hate the sin" says "always love the sinner". It's you relativists who tolerate exceptions—to both. It's you they should fear.

Libby: I don't need to answer that trash talk.

'Isa: Yes you do! It's a serious question: *Why not* be intolerant to any group or individual you choose, if there's no moral absolute?

Libby: Because we've been there, done that, learned from our mistakes. We tried that intolerance and oppression crap in the past, and it didn't work.

'Isa: Oh, but it did—it worked well for the slave owners, and for the Nazis—it was very efficient for them.

Libby: You know, I think I'm rethinking my philosophy of tolerance for everybody. I'm finding you increasingly intolerable.

'Isa: I'm not surprised. The decayed tooth finds the dentist's drill intolerable. No, no, I didn't mean *you're* a decayed tooth. I meant your *arguments* are. Stop looking around for something to throw at me!

Kreeft: Perhaps we should stop for today.

'Isa: Why? It's starting to rain; there's nothing *else* to do for the rest of the afternoon.

Kreeft: Didn't you want to go out for blues? They tell me this is the best weather to catch them, and sunset or sunrise the best time.

Libby: Do we all have to share the same boat?

Kreeft: Every day. It's called Planet Earth.

Libby: I can't take another session this afternoon; I don't even want to do one tonight. Let's fish for fish instead of arguments the rest of the day.

Interview 7

The Arguments from Situations, Intentions, Projection, and Evolution

Libby: Well, here I am back on your rack, your torture chamber. You know, if it wasn't for the great fishing, I think I'd be outta here. The surf hasn't been rideable all week, even at that great secret beach of yours.

Kreeft: It's August. We get rideable surf an average of eight days this month in Lake Atlantic. You should really come back in September: twice as much surf and half as many people.

Libby: Well, the beach was heavenly anyway.

'Isa: And those blues we caught yesterday in the Sound were heavenly blues.

Libby: Are there fish in heaven?

'Isa: Professor Kreeft wrote a book that might answer that question. I think the title was *Everything You Ever Wanted to Know about Heaven but Never Dreamed of Asking*. Right? I don't know whether the fish question comes up, though.

Libby: We really should bring him into this format some time.

Kreeft: Not today, please. You know our agreement. Ten interviews with just the two of you.

Libby: OK, back to work. Where were we?

'Isa: You've got four of your eight arguments left.

Kreeft: Let's see if we can fit them all on one tape this morning. We all ate too much to think last night.

Libby: OK, here we go. I guess I've got to do my job—which is to stick my head in his cannon four more times, and his job is to fire it.

"Cannon to the right of them, cannon to the left of them . . . into the valley of death rode the six hundred." "The Charge of the Light Brigade"—that's me.

So—here's my fifth argument. (I thought it was the sixth. Never mind.) Morality is relative, because even if it *isn't* relative to the individual who makes it up, or to the society that makes the laws—and I still say it is—it's still relative, because it's relative to two other things: changing situations and personal intentions. Even a traditional moralist like you has to admit that. So it's still relative.

'Isa: This is really two arguments, so we should take them one by one, OK?

Libby: OK. But I'm not finished. I didn't give you the arguments yet.

'Isa: If I have to wait as long for the arguments as I had to wait for the bluefish, I'll be starving.

Kreeft: My apologies again for the uncooperative stove.

'Isa: I'm only kidding, Professor. But I still don't understand why we couldn't just barbecue them outdoors.

Kreeft: There's no room. The yard's too tiny. The law says you can't barbecue within ten feet of a house. Look, the tape's running. If you don't get to the arguments, you won't get them all in today. Forget the fish.

'Isa: *Those* fish? Impossible! Even my Papa never caught such fish.

Libby: Come on, let's get down to business. Here's my argument. Morality is relative to situations. And situations are so diverse, and so complex, and so changeable, that—well, it's just unreasonable and unrealistic to say there are rules with no exceptions, ever. That's just not common sense. You want to analyze ordinary moral language? All right, here's a common cliché for you: "The exception proves the rule." It shows that popular opinion admits there are no universal rules with no exceptions. Even "thou shalt not kill"—if there's such a thing as a just war, then *that's* not always true. Sometimes you *have* to kill killers to save innocent lives. And "thou shalt not steal"—if you're dealing with a madman, you'd *better* steal his gun. And lying —if you *don't* lie to a woman and tell her she looks great even when she looks terrible, you're being insensitive and uncharitable. You can always make up some situation where the rule doesn't apply.

'**Isa:** So your argument is that morality is determined by situations, and situations are relative and changing, therefore morality is relative and changing.

Libby: Exactly.

'**Isa:** I think we can save time if we look at your next argument too, at the same time as this one, because I think they have the same logical structure. You said morality is also relative to motive, didn't you?

Libby: Yes. Motive or intention—the subjective factor.

'**Isa:** Well, why don't you summarize that argument now too?

Libby: OK. That's common sense too. We all blame someone for *trying* to murder someone, even if the deed isn't done, simply because the intention is bad. But we don't blame someone for murder if it's accidental, if the deed is done but the intention isn't there. For instance, suppose you give sugar candy to a child who's a serious diabetic, but you have no way of knowing that, and the child dies. You may be a careless person, but you're not a murderer.

'**Isa:** So the argument is that morality is determined by motive, and motive is relative to the individual; therefore morality is relative to the individual.

Libby: Right.

'**Isa:** The two arguments are similar. The only difference is that the argument from situations tries to prove that morality isn't *unchanging* but changing, while the argument from motives tries to prove that morality isn't *objective* but subjective.

Libby: Right. But they both refute absolutism. Morality is relative twice: to situations and to motives.

'**Isa:** Well, since you claim these arguments come from common sense, let me use a commonsense distinction on them. You say morality is *determined* by situations and by motives. I say it's only *conditioned* by situations and motives. It's *partly* determined but not *wholly* determined by those two factors. Commonsense morality—traditional morality—says there are three things that make a human act good or bad: the situation, and the motive, *and the act itself.* How and when and where you do it counts, of course—that's the situation—and *why* you do it counts too—that's the motive—but surely *what you do* counts most of all. You forget that.

Libby: No I don't. Of course what you do counts.

'Isa: But that can still be absolute: the Ten Commandments still hold. They specify *what* to do and what not to do.

Libby: But they're not absolute. Situations and intentions change them.

'Isa: They're still absolute. Situations and intentions don't change them; they just add to them. They don't subtract from them. You need to obey three kinds of commandments, in other words: the Ten Commandments tell you what to do; and commandments about intentions—be unselfish, not selfish, don't be greedy, don't be lustful—tell you what intentions to have; and commandments about situations—be responsible and intelligent and practical—tell you how to apply the rules to different situations. If you disobey any one of the three sets of commandments, you do wrong. All three are absolute—all three are necessary, anyway.

Libby: But "doing the right thing" in the wrong situation changes it to doing the wrong thing. Take charity, for instance. Giving money to the poor is good, but not if the beggar is going to use it to OD on drugs and kill himself. So the situation changes the act from good to bad. And the intention does too: if you give money just to show off, not from any compassion for the poor, that's not good.

'Isa: That's right. But that doesn't mean the Commandments are relative. They tell you what deeds are right and what deeds are wrong. The deed is still right; it's the intention or the situation that's wrong. You forget the deed. There first has to *be* a deed before it can be conditioned by different situations or motives.

Libby: Yeah, but morality is a balancing act, with three balls in the air, not just one. It's like juggling. It's an art, not a science.

'Isa: I agree. But there are rules for each of the three balls. It's like art—the moral life is like art—you're right. It is. A good life is like a good work of art—a good story, for instance. And a good work of art has rules. If it has three aspects, there are rules for all three. *All of the aspects of a work of art have to be good for the art to be good.* A good story has to have a good plot *and* good characterization *and* a good theme. And a good life has to have—you have to do the right thing, the act itself, *and* for the right motive, *and* in the right way, the right circumstances, the right situation. If one of the three goes bad, the art as a whole is bad. A bad plot can make an otherwise good story bad. But a good plot can't make an otherwise bad story good. So a bad intention can make a good deed bad, but a good intention can't make a bad deed good. Killing the rich to feed the poor isn't good, even though the intention may be good. You see? You need all three. You're right: there are three parts, not just one. But all three are necessary. Absolutely necessary.

Libby: Situations aren't absolute. They're relative. And intentions aren't objective. They're subjective.

'Isa: Yes, but situations are not subjective; they're objective. And intentions are not relative—you absolutely must love, not hate, everyone, always. So even "situation ethics" is an *objective* ethics, and even subjectivistic ethics—only a good motive counts—is a *universal and absolute* ethics. You can't get rid of the objective and the universal. Even in situation ethics, it's still objectively right to lie in some situations. And even in subjectivist ethics, the obligation to have good subjective intentions—to love, to be sincere—is an absolute and universal obligation.

Libby: My only absolute is my own private conscience. I'm an individualist.

'Isa: Do you admire someone who *isn't* true to his own private conscience? Do you think it would be right for me deliberately to disobey my conscience?

Libby: No.

'Isa: Then you have a universal ethic, not just an individual one. And is this rule of yours—be true to your conscience—is that rule changing? Do you think it might be right to violate my conscience tomorrow?

Libby: No.

'Isa: Then you have an unchanging rule. And do you think you should obey this rule only when you feel like it and disobey it when you feel like disobeying it?

Libby: No.

'Isa: Then you have an absolute rule—even an objective one. It trumps your subjective feelings.

Libby: But I don't have a list of a lot of absolute "dos" and "don'ts" like you do. I just have one absolute. I'm like a monotheist, and you're like a polytheist. You worship many absolutes.

'Isa: That's silly. A *rule* isn't a *god*. Why do you bring God into it?

Libby: I don't. I'm an agnostic. I don't claim any certainty about God. It was just an analogy.

'Isa: But if you admit the absolute moral authority of your own conscience—if you believe it's never right to disobey your conscience—then you're treating your conscience as God, or else as God's prophet, authorized by God, with divine authority. What gives your conscience that authority, if not God? Where did your conscience come from, if it's not God's prophet in your soul?

Libby: It evolved, with the rest of us. It came from the apes, like everything else in us. And then it's conditioned by society, like everything else in us.

'Isa: What gives the apes such an authority? What gives society such an authority? Are apes or other people infallible?

Libby: Of course not.

'Isa: Then why do you treat them as if they were? If conscience is the voice of King Kong, not King God, why obey it?

Libby: Are you saying an agnostic can't respect her conscience?

'Isa: No, I'm saying someone who respects her conscience can't be an agnostic.

Libby: Look, let's argue about God some other time. We're talking about human deeds and motives today. And I'm saying morality is in the motive.

'Isa: And I'm agreeing with you, and then adding that motives are always naturally connected to deeds, as arms are connected to hands, or acorns are connected to oak trees. Some deeds *can't* come from good motives—like rape—and some motives naturally produce good deeds: love produces philanthropy. Good trees, good fruit; bad trees, bad fruit. You can't isolate motives from deeds. Or situations either.

Libby: That's true. But that's my point: every deed and every motive is always embedded in some concrete situation. But situations are relative. You can't go by some simple, inflexible yardstick in this world. It's always changing.

'Isa: Yes it is, but the principles aren't. So you have to apply the same principles to different situations. The very fact that you have to take the situation into account, as you said—the very fact that you have to apply the same principles differently to different situations— presupposes the validity of those principles, rather than eliminating the principles or undermining them.

Libby: But you absolutists tend to absolutize your applications as well as your principles.

'Isa: We shouldn't. There's no need to.

Libby: Isn't there a natural tension, though, in our minds between the unchanging absolutes and the changing situations? The mind tends to prefer one to the other. It's hard to do justice to both. And it's much easier to go for the absolute and sit there, feeling secure.

'Isa: There shouldn't be such a tension. There needn't be. In fact, as an absolutist I feel no fear of changing situations. I've got my absolutes; I have no need to absolutize relative things. I can sit light on them. It's you relativists who yearn for absolutes—you miss them— and so you naturally idolize some relative thing. You can't condemn adultery, or abortion, so you condemn smoking. Or guns. Or pollution.

Libby: Our yardsticks are flexible. Yours are rigid. And that makes *you* rigid.

'Isa: I agree we shouldn't be rigid. But our principles should be. We should *apply* our standards flexibly; but if the standard is as flexible as the situation, it's no standard at all.

Libby: That's just an abstract logical argument. In the real world . . .

'Isa: In the real world, you can't measure an eel with another eel. You need a rigid ruler to measure a squirming thing—a thing like the modern world.

Libby: You sound so damned sure of yourself, so dogmatic, so judgmental! Your namesake said, "Judge not." But you don't dig that soft stuff, do you?

'Isa: What do you think Jesus meant when he said "judge not"? Do you think he meant "don't judge deeds, don't believe the Commandments, don't morally discriminate a just war from an unjust war or a hero from a bully"? He couldn't have meant that. He meant "don't claim to judge motives and hearts, which only God can see". I can judge your deeds, because I can see them. I can't judge what your motives are, because I can't see that.

Libby: Then stop being so judgmental about that, at least.

'Isa: But I can judge what your motives *ought* to be—just as you're doing, when you judge "judgmentalism".

Libby: Yeah, I stand by that.

'Isa: But you have no *ground* for that. Only the moral absolutist can condemn judgmentalism and intolerance. You relativists condemn only one thing: moral absolutists.

Libby: No, moral absolutism. Love the sinner, hate the sin, remember?

'Isa: But that's our distinction, not yours. You say there are no objective absolutes; you reduce the sin to the sinner, the objective to the subjective. So you have to either condemn sinners along with sins or else love sins along with sinners.

Libby: What right do you have to tell me what I have to do?

'Isa: I think we're getting personal again instead of logical. Do you have any other defense of your argument about situations and motives, or should we look at the next argument?

Libby: The next one, please. And this one's right up your alley, Professor: it's from a philosopher—David Hume. I read this back in college, and it made a lot of sense to me, so I'm anxious to see how you try to refute it. I think Hume's argument was the basis for what you called, in our earlier interview, the "emotive theory of values"— that the only possible *locus* for moral values is our subjective feelings, not objective facts, because the only qualities we can observe in the objective world are colors and sizes and shapes and quantities and events and energy and things of that sort that appear to our external senses. Values don't appear there; they don't come from the outside world because there's no door through which they can come. Our five senses are the five doors, and values don't come through any of those doors. You can't see a value, or hear one, or smell one. So they must come from within. We think they come from without because we do unconscious projecting all the time—just as we project the blue color of a pair of blue-tinted sunglasses out onto the world, and we think the world is blue. The empirical facts are black and white, and we color these facts with our own value-colored feelings.

I think Hume gives the example of a murder. You see a maniac murder a little old lady. What do you see? You see facts, but you don't see values. You *feel* values. You feel repulsed, or repugnant, you feel bad about the fact. And you unconsciously project your feeling onto the act, or onto the murderer. So you call the act bad, or the murderer bad. But it's projection. "Badness" can't inhere in a physical act, as color does, or size, or shape. You can't discover badness or goodness by observation, as you can discover colors or shapes.

And that's why we differ about values, why we *argue* about good and evil: we feel differently about the same act. Hume's theory explains why we can't agree about morality, as we can about physics. It explains everything so simply that once you see it, you say, "Oh, obviously. Why didn't I see that before?"

And then the later philosophers, the analytic philosophers, explained why we didn't see it, how language deceives us. "That deed is a terrible deed!" we say. But if we wanted to be literal, we should say, "I feel terrible when I see that deed."

'Isa: Yes, that is a very popular theory among the philosophers. But I think it's weakest right where it seems to be strongest: it seems to explain our moral experience so easily, but it doesn't. It centers on the idea of projection: that we are, as you say, unconsciously projecting our own personal feelings out onto the objective deed. But that simply doesn't match our experience. Look here: you see a murder. You call it evil. Why? You say because you first feel evil in yourself and then unconsciously project it out onto the deed. Well, I can't prove you're wrong about the unconscious part, because the unconscious isn't conscious! By definition, it's what we're *not* conscious of. But I can prove you're wrong about the conscious part. You say you first feel evil in yourself, then you unconsciously project it onto the deed. But you *don't* feel evil in yourself when you see a murder. You feel nausea, or physical sickness maybe; but the moral feeling you have isn't evil. If anything, it's self-righteousness. You feel good next to a murderer, not evil. You feel evil next to a saint or in the presence of God, not in the presence of a murderer.

Libby: But *of course* the feeling is in us. Where else could it be? Out there somewhere? That's silly.

'Isa: The *act* of feeling is in us—the "to feel"—of course. Just as the act of seeing and the act of thinking is. But seeing and thinking are *intentional*: they intend objects; they're *about* something objective. And so is feeling—some feelings, anyway. What do you feel when you see a murder? You feel the evil of the *murderer*, or of the act of murder. You don't feel *you're* evil.

And here's a second weakness in your argument. It assumes a theory of knowledge that simply isn't true: that your only access to objective truth is through the five senses. Technically, that's Empiricism, or extreme empiricism.

Libby: Prove it. Prove Empiricism is false.

'Isa: That's easy. How tall is your body?

Libby: Five foot six.

'Isa: Are you conscious of that fact?

Libby: Of course.

'Isa: So you are also conscious of your consciousness of that fact, because you just told me you were conscious of it.

Libby: Yes . . .

'Isa: How tall is your consciousness?

Libby: Hmmph. But suppose my consciousness is just my body's brain working and not some invisible spiritual thing? Maybe there is no "soul".

'Isa: Then you are just a body?

Libby: Yes.

'Isa: Then what is the "you" that possesses that body? You call it "your" body.

Libby: OK, OK, I see: self-consciousness isn't just empirical. But that's subjective. I still say our only knowledge of objective reality is empirical.

'Isa: Do you know what kind of a person I am?

Libby: Yeah, a smart-ass professor.

'Isa: Do you know something about my mind? My personality? My feelings?

Libby: Yes, alas . . .

'Isa: It's a different mind than yours, right? And you know that, right? But it's not a colored thing, made of molecules. So you do know some things that are objective to you—other people's minds—even though they don't come in through the five sense doors.

Libby: But I know them only through what I hear you say with my ears.

'Isa: Of course. But what you know is not just what you hear. You infer, or deduce, or conclude, or suspect, or intuit something about my mind from what you hear with your ears.

Libby: Suppose there's no difference between the mind and what we sense. Maybe there's no "soul" that's more than the bodily senses.

'Isa: Then how could you be wrong about it? How could you think different things about my mind than the things that are really there? For instance, if you hear me insulting one of your arguments, you infer that I'm insulting you and have a low opinion of you. And you're wrong. You hear rightly, but you think wrongly. So there is something really there—my mind, with its thoughts, including my opinion of you—something that you don't sense with any of your five senses, but that you do know, or can know. If you can be wrong about it, you can be right about it, you can know it.

Libby: And what do you think that proves?

'Isa: That Empiricism is false. That your argument uses a false premise.

Libby: I can't believe you think you've refuted a respectable philosophical theory in two minutes.

'Isa: I can do it in *one* minute. Here's an even easier refutation of Empiricism: it's self-contradictory. It says all our knowledge is by sense perception, but Empiricism itself can't be known by sense perception.

Libby: Why not?

'Isa: Because none of its terms is empirically observable. Knowledge is only perception, is it? What color is knowledge? Or the act of perception? What senses do we use to sense the act of sensing?

Libby: But the scientific method works, and it works by Empiricism —I mean, by restricting your data to the empirical. "I feel the vibrations from an alien intelligence"—that's not scientific data. "I see four satellites around Jupiter"—that is.

'Isa: Yes, that method works—it's worked so well in understanding the physical dimensions of reality that we're naturally tempted to extend it to all the dimensions, including the moral. But that's really stupid.

Libby: Why "really stupid"?

'Isa: Not only is it morally stupid, morally destructive, destructive of morality, but it's logically stupid too because it's self-contradictory.

Libby: The scientific method is self-contradictory? This I gotta hear: science is self-contradictory!

'Isa: No, not the scientific method but the idea that it's the only one. Not science but scientism.

Libby: And how is this self-contradictory?

'Isa: It amounts to saying that whatever can't be proved by the scientific method can't be proved at all. But *that* statement can't be proved by the scientific method. Therefore it can't be proved at all.

Libby: Maybe not "*proved* by the scientific method", just "*discovered* by the scientific method".

'Isa: Same argument. Whatever can't be discovered by the scientific method can't be discovered at all—but that fact can't be discovered by the scientific method.

Libby: Yeah, yeah, I see that. So where did the "emotivist theory of value" go wrong, according to you? What's wrong with trusting your eyes too much?

'Isa: It went wrong because it trusted the eyes too *little*—the inner eyes. It's a failure of insight, a failure to "just see" right and wrong where they are: in people and acts. An Empiricist like Hume reduces all "seeing" to physical seeing. Why? He could never physically see that this is true; and 99% of all good and wise and sane human beings throughout history have claimed to *intuitively* see that it's *not* true.

Libby: So you're appealing to intuition now, not logic?

'Isa: Yes. That's how we first "see" right and wrong. It's called "conscience".

Libby: The inner eye, eh?

'Isa: Yes. Just as we just "see" the beauty of the stars with the inner eye and see the light of the stars with the outer eye. Or we "see" the trustworthiness of a good friend with the inner eye and the shape of his body with the outer eye. Or we "see" the triviality of a paper clip and the greatness of a great work of art or a great deed. That's how we "see" right and wrong. It's simply an arbitrary prejudice to exclude that inner seeing, that nonphysical seeing. It just doesn't square with experience. And it's inhuman. It reduces humans to cameras.

Libby: Well, I guess it's time to run my last argument by you. It's a suicide mission, I know. But frankly, I'm fascinated by how you take two minutes to tear apart theories it took scientists and philosophers two centuries to construct. You're really good at destruction, Professor. Do you call yourself one of those . . . what do they call them? Deconstructionists?

'Isa: God forbid! I'd rather be called an honest Mafia hit man.

Libby: Maybe you should consider making a little extra money on the side that way. You've got a real talent for destruction there.

'**Isa:** The talent for destruction isn't in me; it's in your theory, relativism. It has big holes in it, holes it should be easy to see. But come on, let's see your last argument. Is it supposed to be "scientific" like the last few?

Libby: It sure is. It's based on evolution.

'**Isa:** Evolution? What do fossils have to do with the moral law?

Libby: Evolution explains morality, quite simply and adequately as an evolutionary survival device. It's the "survival of the fittest". Those groups that developed morality survived. They cooperated. They behaved in ways we now call "moral"—justly and charitably and socially and honestly—all that made them more fit to survive. The tribes that konked each other on the head just died off. Natural selection discriminated between morality and immorality, that's all. Not God, not Moses, just evolution.

'**Isa:** So you have a nice little simple theory instead of my big, mysterious one.

Libby: That's what science is, Professor. Ockham's Razor, remember?

'**Isa:** I'd love to explore why you prefer the simple to the mysterious —it's technically called "reductionism"—but I think we're scheduled to cover that next time, as part of the interview on the sources of relativism. So let me just refute your last objection to absolutism now, which is that morality is nothing but a biological survival instinct. OK?

Libby: Refute away, O refuter!

'**Isa:** You're violating a basic law of metaphysics . . .

Libby: Oh, metaphysics now, is it? We're refuting science through metaphysics? How sober, and scientific, and modern! Hey, let me tell the world that whoever hears these tapes is going to be privileged to hear one of the finest minds of the thirteenth century!

'**Isa:** You just paid me an undeserved compliment, Libby. You put me in the same class as Saint Thomas Aquinas. No, not metaphysics in the sense you mean it—the "occult" section in California bookstores —but metaphysics in the traditional sense, the sober science of the basic principles that all reality conforms to, like the law of causality. Very scientific and sober.

Libby: So what's in my theory that's not scientific and sober?

'Isa: Your idea violates a basic law of all science, the law of causality, because it puts more in the effect than in the cause; it gets more out of less, gets something out of nothing.

Libby: How?

'Isa: It gets the moral out of the nonmoral. Your theory says that morality evolved from something nonmoral. That says there's more in the effect than in the cause. The cause is only biological, not moral; but the effect is moral.

Libby: But we *do* get more out of less, all the time.

'Isa: Show me one example.

Libby: You! You're bigger, and older, and fatter than you used to be. You might even be wiser (though that's really stretching it).

'Isa: That's only growth.

Libby: Sure, but it gives you bigger effects from smaller causes.

'Isa: No, not if you look at all the causes. The little child plus all the food he eats plus all the instructions from parents and teachers equals the big adult. The *Mona Lisa* isn't caused by Da Vinci's brush. The brush is only Da Vinci's instrument. There's more in *him* than in the *Mona Lisa*.

Libby: What about your brain producing thoughts right now?

'Isa: Same thing. The brain is the *instrument* of the mind, as the brush is the instrument of Da Vinci's mind and body together.

Libby: Here we go back to ghosts. I knew we'd get to that California bookstore eventually!

'Isa: My mind is not a ghost, Libby. Speak for yourself about yours.

Libby: Ooh, how very scientific and logical our interview has become!

'**Isa:** Can we get back to the argument, please? The point is simply that your theory violates the law of causality. You try to explain morality by matter, the conscious by the unconscious.

Libby: Hey, Professor, did you ever hear of the theory of evolution? I guess they didn't teach that in the thirteenth century, huh?

'**Isa:** I have no problem with evolution.

Libby: But it says more came from less, mind from matter.

'**Isa:** No it doesn't. It can't. I'll prove it to you. Tell me: Evolution is a theory in which science?

Libby: Biology.

'**Isa:** And biology is an empirical science, right? Its data are observable by the senses?

Libby: Right.

'**Isa:** And brains and nervous systems and bodies are all observable biological data, right?

Libby: Right.

'**Isa:** But what you call metaphysics isn't?

Libby: Right. No spooks for me.

'**Isa:** No spirits, or souls, or immaterial minds?

Libby: Right.

'**Isa:** Then how could the theory of evolution claim to explain *minds*?

Libby: Did I say it did?

'**Isa:** You said evolution explained that *mind* came from *matter*.

Libby: Oh.

'**Isa:** You see, the biological world is like a gigantic pen. It's not a mind, but it writes a beautiful and intelligent and meaningful letter: the human brain, a superintelligently designed computer. So that pen must be held by the hand of a superintelligent writer.

Libby: God, you mean?

'Isa: Yes. Evolution is one of the best arguments for the existence of God that I've ever seen.

Libby: But this "cosmic writer" is invisible. Science can't verify her.

'Isa: That's true. So what? What logically follows from that?

Libby: Uh—I don't know. I lost the thread of the argument. Make your point again, please. And could you minus the metaphysics? I can follow simple logic, but metaphysics messes me up.

'Isa: Fine. Your theory violates a simple logical law because it puts more in the conclusion than in the premises. It tries to generate a moral conclusion, a conclusion that has "ought" in it, from merely factual premises, premises that have no "ought" but only "is".

Libby: Show me. How does my theory do that?

'Isa: Your theory is that morality is explainable as an instrument for biological survival, right? The tribes that stopped bashing each other on the head survived, and those that didn't stop killed each other. And so we descended from the successful tribes that practiced morality, and cooperation, and altruism. That's it, isn't it?

Libby: Yes.

'Isa: Now let's take a concrete example of a moral act. Take heroism, to the point of martyrdom. One individual risks his life to save a whole community or his family. You say this is morally good because it's biologically necessary to save the community, right?

Libby: Right.

'Isa: So you seem to get your "ought" conclusion—that heroism ought to be done, that it's moral—from an "is" premise—that it's necessary for biological survival.

Libby: That's right.

'Isa: But if you know your logic, you know that that argument lacks a major premise. To be logically valid, it has to assume this premise: that *whatever is necessary for biological survival ought to be done*. Whatever is necessary for survival ought to be done; and heroism is necessary for survival; therefore heroism ought to be done.

Libby: OK, so I assume that. That's a true assumption. What's the problem?

'Isa: The problem is that that's a *moral* assumption. You're not getting morality in your conclusion from merely factual premises; you're beginning with a moral premise. And you have to, or else you can't get a moral conclusion. So morality has to be primary, not derivative.

Libby: Hmm. You're the logic teacher, I guess. I don't think your argument is going to impress many people, though: it's very abstract. Whereas my idea—evolution and how morality evolved—is concrete. People can understand that.

'Isa: Then let me be concrete too. Let me appeal to experience. Your reduction of morality to instinct contradicts not only logic but experience.

Libby: I'm all ears. Exactly what are you going to try to prove by experience?

'Isa: That we don't experience morality as we experience any instinct.

Libby: Show me the difference.

'Isa: Instincts and desires "push" us from within, from our own nature, don't they?

Libby: Yes.

'Isa: But morality "pulls" us from without, from something outside of us.

Libby: Not from atoms and molecules.

'Isa: No, but from the real, objective situation.

Libby: In other words, the world. Atoms and molecules.

'Isa: There's more in the situation than atoms and molecules. There's good and evil. There are persons. There are souls, minds, wills, spirits, feelings, thoughts.

Libby: I thought you were going to be concrete and specific and appeal to experience. You're back in metaphysics.

'Isa: OK, here, take this experience. Let's say you promised your friend yesterday that you'd help her move her furniture this morning, because she has to have it all out by noon. But you were up until 3:00 A.M., and when the alarm goes off this morning you feel dead tired. At that moment you experience two things: the *desire* to go back to sleep and the *obligation* to get up to fulfill your promise. Now just look at how different those two experiences are. You don't experience any obligation to sleep at all, and you don't experience any desire to get up. You're moved in one way by your desire for sleep and in another way—a very different way—by morality, by what you think you ought to do. I see you're following this so far. OK, now how do your feelings come to you? Don't they seem to come from the inside out, so to speak? But your moral obligation comes to you from the outside in—from your friend, and the situation, and the real relationship between that objective situation and you.

Libby: I follow that.

'Isa: Now, you have to do one of two things: either get up or stay in bed. If you shut off the alarm and go back to bed, you're obeying your biological desire for sleep. But if you get up and help your friend, you're obeying a different kind of thing altogether.

Libby: I see that. But that "different kind of thing altogether" doesn't necessarily have to be some absolute, objective, universal thing, your transcendent moral law. Not everybody believes in that.

'Isa: What is it that you're obeying, then?

Libby: My conscience.

'Isa: And what is your conscience telling you?

Libby: That I ought to help my friend.

'Isa: So you're responding to what your conscience perceives, not what your eyes or nerve endings perceive.

Libby: That's right.

'Isa: You're responding to the perceived moral quality of the deed of fulfilling your promise and refusing the perceived immoral quality of the deed of—what's the phrase? Welshing on your promise? Ratting on your promise?

Libby: True. But why can't that just be my own deeper desire to be just?

'**Isa:** Because what you perceive as morally right "pulls" you from without, contrary to your desire to sleep, while your desires push you from within, from your own nature. The moral obligation moves you as an end, a goal, an ideal—what Aristotle called a "final cause". The desire moves you as a beginning, a push—what Aristotle called an "efficient cause".

Libby: But why can't conscience be just another instinct, a stronger instinct that takes over and pushes out the instinct to sleep?

'**Isa:** Well, for one thing, it *isn't* usually stronger, but weaker. The desire you have to be sociable and feel good while you're helping your friend—the "herd instinct", biologists call it, I think—that's not going to be as strong as the desire to sleep when you're really, really tired. Or—take another case—you see somebody being mugged. Your desire to help him, your "herd instinct", is probably going to be weaker, feel weaker, than your desire for self-preservation, especially if you see the mugger has a big knife. Right?

Libby: Right.

'**Isa:** But you might go help him anyway.

Libby: Not if I'm afraid of that knife!

'**Isa:** No, you might do it anyway. Some people would. I think you would. You did some pretty courageous things when you were a social worker, didn't you?

Libby: Maybe that was just a deeper instinct.

'**Isa:** No, that was your conscience.

Libby: All right, so I call my conscience my moral instinct. You don't. That's just a matter of words.

'**Isa:** No. It's a real difference. Instincts are many; conscience is one. Instincts are disordered; conscience is orderly. Instincts are like a hundred animals at a zoo. They need a keeper, a principle of order. Instincts are like keys on a piano. You need a piece of sheet music to tell you what keys to play at what time. The instincts contradict each other. "Follow your instincts" is nonsense—which instincts? But "follow your conscience" is not nonsense.

Libby: I think I see the difference.

'**Isa:** Here's another way to see it. No instinct is absolutely right, is it?

Libby: Not for a relativist.

'**Isa:** And not for an absolutist either. Sometimes we have to encourage our instinct for survival, or for patriotism, or for family, or for sex, and sometimes we have to discourage those instincts. It all depends on the situation.

Libby: Do you agree with that?

'**Isa:** Of course.

Libby: But that's relativism.

'**Isa:** Only of instincts. Not of conscience. And I think you're an absolutist too where conscience is concerned. Didn't you admit the other day that you believed it was never morally right deliberately to disobey your own conscience?

Libby: Yes, I do believe that. But my conscience tells me different things in different situations and different things than your conscience tells you.

'**Isa:** Maybe so, but do you say I'm morally right if I do what my conscience tells me is wrong?

Libby: No.

'**Isa:** So conscience should always be obeyed. But no instinct should always be obeyed. Therefore conscience is not an instinct.

Libby: Wow, that is logical.

'**Isa:** And I've saved the simplest argument for last. Morality can't be a survival instinct because sometimes it doesn't help us survive at all. Self-sacrifice for some transcendent, otherworldly goal—being a martyr—how does that help you survive? Spending time and money and energy taking care of the weak and the poor and the handicapped and the elderly—is that survival-efficient?

Libby: Just the opposite, it seems. OK, the tape's ending, and so are my arguments.

Kreeft: But the rain isn't. Do you want to do the next tape this afternoon?

Libby: All right. Just give me a little time to prepare for it.

Interview 8

The Roots of Relativism: Reductionism

Libby: Our topic for this afternoon is supposed to be not relativism but its roots. Not its historical roots—we did that in the third interview—but its logical roots. That's how you wanted to set it up, right?

'Isa: Yes.

Libby: And you feel this is necessary—we should do a whole interview about this—because . . . ?

'Isa: Because a good gardener knows it's not enough just to tear up weeds; you have to expose and tear up their roots too.

Libby: A weed, now—that's our label of the day for relativism, I see. Well, let it never be said that the professor substituted arguing for name calling.

'Isa: Arguing? What else did we do on the last two tapes? We examined all your arguments yesterday, remember? Eight of them. Do you have any more?

Libby: Would I like to stick my head in your lion's mouth a few more times? No thank you.

'Isa: Well, then, let's get to the next topic. We have to find the philosophical roots of relativism and do to them the same thing we did to relativism.

Libby: A good spanking?

'Isa: A logical refutation.

Libby: Seriously, Professor, would it be too much to ask for your psychological analysis too? Of both relativism and its root, whatever that turns out to be?

'Isa: Reductionism, in a word. That's the philosophical root of relativism.

Libby: Well, if those two monsters are as ugly as you say they are, if relativism is like Grendel and reductionism is like Grendel's mother, and you're going to be Beowulf and slay these two monsters, then I'd like to know why do so many people see these bad guys as good guys and you absolutists as the monsters? You really ought to have some reasonable account of what makes relativism and reductionism attractive to people like me who are a bit more intelligent and responsible than a mass murderer.

'Isa: A fair question. I'll try to answer that too.

Libby: Thank you.

'Isa: So we need to do two things today. We already refuted relativism, but not its root, reductionism. So we need to define and refute reductionism. And then we need to answer your other question, why it seems so attractive. I'm happy to accept your challenge to do a psychological analysis too, not just a logical one, and look at the _motives_ for reductionism.

Libby: And I'll bet you've got some dark suspicions in your back pocket to give me as answers to that question.

'Isa: Well, the first one is not dark at all but very plain and out in the open already. We went over it earlier, on the third tape—Ockham's Razor. Remember?

Libby: Sure. "Entities should not be multiplied beyond necessity." Or, "Always use the simplest possible explanation." Now what do you say was the motive behind that principle?

'Isa: Utility. It's an economic principle for science.

Libby: So what's wrong with it?

'Isa: Nothing, for science, but everything for life. Science isn't life. If you're doing the practical science of brain surgery on your grandmother, it may be useful and efficient to think of her body simply as a computer—I mean, of her brain simply as a computer, and her body as a machine. But not when you bring her home to live with you.

Libby: That makes sense. So what's the lesson here?

'Isa: That we shouldn't confuse a good method with good metaphysics. We shouldn't confuse the useful narrowing of a mental perspective with a real narrowness in the thing.

Libby: That also makes sense.

'Isa: Because it has a sound psychological basis: the fact that we can't usually think very clearly about two aspects of the same complex object at the same time. Especially when that object is a person, and especially a person we care about.

Libby: What aspects are you thinking of?

'Isa: The soul and the brain, for instance, or religion and chemistry, or economics and aesthetics.

Libby: OK.

'Isa: But that psychological fact about our limitations does *not* mean that any one of those aspects that we have to distinguish and separate is less real than another.

Libby: OK. Is that it? Nothing sounds very controversial there.

'Isa: But there's the error that's the first motive for reductionism: confusing method and metaphysics.

Libby: OK. Next?

'Isa: A second error that leads to reductionism is based on this same fact that things have many different aspects, or dimensions. Aristotle long ago classified these as basically four: the "four causes", philosophers call them, the four kinds of explanations of anything at all . . .

Libby: I know those, but go ahead. Explain them for the tape.

'Isa: The *material cause* is the raw material of the effect, its contents, what it's made of—its potential to be formed. The material cause of this house is wood. The *formal cause* is the nature or essence of the effect, what it *is*, or what it's made *to be*. It's the actualization of the potential. The formal cause of this house is that it's a summer cottage. The *efficient cause* is the agent that produces the effect, or changes it, if the effect is an action; what it's made *by*. The efficient cause of this house is the carpenter. Finally, the *final cause* is the end or good or goal or purpose of the effect, what it's made *for*. The final cause of this house is to live in during the summer.

Libby: Now how does this apply to reductionism?

'Isa: It gives us two fundamentally different kinds of explanation: by material causes or by formal causes, by efficient causes or by final causes. Reductionism accepts only material and efficient causes. For instance, in Plato's *Phaedo* . . .

Libby: That's the account of Socrates' death in prison, isn't it?

'Isa: Yes. There we see Socrates sitting in prison, and his disciples ask him why he's there. They've bribed the guards, and he can escape. (You know, actually, this might be the *Crito*, not the *Phaedo*. I'm not sure.) He asks them *why* it is that he doesn't escape. Is it because his muscles and bones hold him in his chair? That's how a purely material explanation would put it, the kind of explanation Socrates found in previous philosophers, the "pre-Socratics"—Anaxagoras, I think, is the one he quotes. These philosophers spoke only of material and efficient causes: earth, air, fire, and water, and the forces of attraction and repulsion. A simple explanation. A reductionistic explanation. But it won't work. Socrates argues that if that was all there was, he would not be sitting there. To explain why he sits there you have to bring in the final cause, the purpose. And that is his moral conviction that no one should do a bad deed even for a good end, that the end does not justify the means. He thinks it's wrong to disobey the law, even when the law is wrong. Whether that belief of his is right or wrong, that's the cause of his sitting in prison. You see? The reductionistic explanation doesn't always explain things. There are some dimensions of reality that can't be considered by the scientific method, because that method ignores final causes, and morality is in that realm: final causality, purpose, good.

Libby: But Socrates and Plato and Aristotle and their medieval followers didn't use the scientific method, and that's why they weren't very good scientists compared to the moderns, precisely because they wouldn't use what you call reductionism. Only in the Renaissance do you get the scientific method, and only then does science really start to progress by leaps and bounds. That method has to be the greatest discovery in the history of science, because it opens all the other doors, like a skeleton key. The ancients didn't have it, the moderns do.

'Isa: Oh, I think you're right there—though I'd add that the key to the key is math, exact measurement. But I think you're also wrong, because you're making the same mistake the ancients did: you're confusing science and philosophy. They tried to do science by using a philosophical method, and you're trying to do philosophy by using the scientific method: the same confusion in reverse. Both the ancients and the moderns forget how different science and philosophy are. The scientific method is based on this psychological fact: that if we shut one eye—the eye that sees final and formal causes, purposes and essences—then we can map what we see with the other eye very clearly—the material and efficient causes. But good philosophy does exactly the opposite: it keeps all eyes open. It focuses on the things science ignores, rightly ignores, has to ignore, especially final causes.

Libby: And why do you have to focus on final causes to be a good philosopher?

'Isa: Because, as Aristotle said, the final cause is the first of causes and the cause of all the other causes, the reason why all the others work. For instance, why are candles made of wax rather than stone? Why do they have that material cause? That material cause is explained only by the final cause: that candles are designed for burning. And eyes are made of optic nerves because they're designed for seeing. So the material cause is explained by the final cause. And the efficient cause is explained by the final cause too. The carpenter saws the board *because* he's making a boat out of it. The seed pushes up through the soil *because* it's growing into a plant.

Libby: And why doesn't the modern scientist talk like that? Why doesn't the scientific method deal with final causality?

'Isa: Because final causality isn't a physical thing. It's mental and spiritual. Purposes and ends and goals and goods and designs have no color or shape. They come from minds, not molecules—though they make a difference to molecules. You can see the *results* of design in the intricacy of the cell, or the atom, but you can't see design itself; that's an idea, a plan; it's in the mind. So if there's final causality, there must be mind. And if the final cause is the primal cause, then mind must be primary.

Libby: So mind is primary to matter. Mind over matter.

'Isa: Yes.

Libby: That sounds more like California metaphysics than modern science.

'Isa: "California metaphysics"? The four causes don't work only in California. In fact, if there's anywhere they *don't* work, it's probably California.

Libby: Greek metaphysics, then. Ancient Greek metaphysics. You're defending Aristotle over Einstein, right?

'Isa: No, I see no contradiction between Aristotle's metaphysics and Einstein's physics, only between Aristotle's physics and Einstein's physics. But I do see a contradiction between Aristotle's metaphysics and modern metaphysics, and I think the moderns are as wrong in metaphysics as the ancients were in physics.

Libby: So there is a real controversy.

'Isa: Yes. You could call it a clash of world views. Modern materialism versus ancient common sense.

Libby: But modern materialism works. It's the scientific method.

'Isa: No, what works is the method, not the "ism". An "ism" is more than a method. An "ism" is a metaphysics. There's nothing wrong with the scientific method and nothing wrong with reductionism there. Reductionism is right for the method but not for the metaphysics.

Libby: So how did the method take over the metaphysics? Which scientists do you say made the mistake?

'Isa: Not scientists; philosophers. When modern philosophers claimed exclusivity for the scientific method, that led to materialistic metaphysics, and the world view that turns reality inside out, with matter as primary, explaining mind, surrounding mind. Mind is reduced to matter then. The mind is reduced to the brain.

Libby: And that's reductionism. Reducing the mysterious mind to simple matter.

'Isa: Yes. Although matter is turning out to be a lot less simple and more mysterious than anyone thought.

Libby: And the alternative "'ism'", the world view you prefer, is . . . ?

'Isa: The other world view is the opposite: matter is surrounded by mind, there because of mind, explained by mind.

Libby: In other words, there must be a God behind evolution to design it? Isn't that the same question more concretely?

'Isa: Essentially, yes. Reductionism says our minds are an accidental belch of the mindless primordial slime, and I say that the whole physical universe, from the Big Bang to our discovery of the Big Bang, is a work of art dreamed up by a cosmic mind. It's like a play: there are two ways to look at it. You can see the material setting as surrounding and explaining everything else in the play, or else you can see it as one of the aspects of the play, surrounded by the play and explained by the play as a whole. The universe is like an enormous stage. All the matter in the universe is like the physical setting for a play that has a plot and a theme and a meaning and a design from the mind of its Author. And *that* explains the setting, not vice versa. And that play is human life, and the plot or point of the play is not the scenery but the moral choices of the characters, choices between good and evil. That's the drama of the universe.

Libby: That sounds rather charming, but . . . rather mythological. Why don't we usually see the universe that way any more? Isn't it because science and reductionism have worked better?

'Isa: No. It's because we've lost the ability to read signs.

Libby: Whatever do you mean?

'Isa: The ancients were well versed in two kinds of thought: seeing the meaning as well as seeing the matter, reading the significance of the sign as well as staring at it. You could call one the inner eye and the other the outer eye. For the last few centuries we've specialized so much in seeing the matter that we've ignored the meaning, and forgotten how to see it. We've stood there looking *at* things so long that we've forgotten how to look *along* things, as you look along a sign and look at what it signifies, at its significance. We've forgotten that *things* are also *signs*.

Libby: So science is the art of thing reading, and philosophy is the art of sign reading?

'Isa: Very well put.

Libby: Let's talk more about evolution, if you don't mind. I think that's the main reason why modern scientists and modern educated people prefer the world view you call reductionism. We've explained things so much more successfully that way: great oaks come from little acorns, and men from apes. (*Humans* from apes. Sorry; I'm slipping into your male chauvinist language. You see, it's much more obvious that men came from apes than women. You guys are still going around thumping your chest and conquering territory most of the time.) Seriously, reductionism *works*, especially in biology. Whether there's a divine mind behind it or not, we can explain the higher life forms by the lower, and it works very well. Natural selection is all you need. And that's an example of reductionism, isn't it?

'Isa: Yes. But it isn't all you need. It leaves something out. Great oaks do come from little acorns, but you forgot that the little acorns came from great oaks to begin with. And maybe men did evolve from apes, but you forgot that that very explanation of apes came from men.

Libby: But the *apes* didn't come from men. Men didn't say one day, "Let's take our clothes off and walk on all fours and climb trees and eat bananas", and gradually evolve into apes. Everything came from natural selection.

'Isa: If natural selection is a fact, it's not evidence for reductionism but for a divine mind behind it. The effect has to have an adequate cause. If you see balloons evolving into biplanes and then into jets and then rocket ships, you know there's got to be a mind designing the whole series. And there is, of course: the human mind. So if you see slime pools producing salamanders and then woolly mammoths and then lawyers, you know there's got to be a cosmic mind behind it.

Libby: But . . . natural selection explains everything without a God.

'Isa: It explains the "how", but not the "why". It's like the gears and wheels of a clock.

Libby: Hmm . . . so you prefer expansionism to reductionism.

'Isa: That's a good label. But it's not just personal preference. It's more reasonable.

Libby: Why?

'Isa: Because reductionism tries to explain *Hamlet* by counting the syllables. Expansionism explains the syllables by *Hamlet*. Reductionism tries to explain the cathedral by its stones; expansionism explains the stones by the cathedral. Which is the more reasonable explanation?

Libby: Hmm. So is that your argument against reductionism?

'Isa: Oh, no. I haven't even started that yet. I've just been looking at the sources of it. You want a refutation? I have two. A logical one and a practical one.

Libby: I'm listening.

'Isa: The logical refutation of reductionism is that it is self-contradictory.

Libby: Somehow, I thought you'd say that.

'Isa: For one thing, there's the point I made yesterday about accepting only what can be proved by the scientific method: that principle itself can't be proved by the scientific method. But there's another argument, a more strictly logical argument, based on the logical structure of a reductionist proposition. To express reductionism in a proposition, that proposition must take the form "S is only P", or "S is nothing but P". "There is no more than P in S." "There is no more-than-P S." That's a universal negative proposition. Now for you to know the truth of a universal negative proposition, you have to know absolutely everything about S . . .

Libby: Wait. I followed you up to that point, but why do you have to know everything about S to say S is nothing but P?

'Isa: To be sure that there isn't something more in S, in some area of S, or some aspect or division or dimension of S, or some example of S somewhere, that you didn't know, that has something more than P in it.

Libby: I need an example.

'Isa: Try this: "Men are nothing but apes." Suppose you mean that metaphorically: that men act like apes—chest thumping, territorial, whatever your favorite stereotype. Say you've met a thousand men, and they all act that way. But there may be a man somewhere that you've never met that's not that way. You're being too dogmatic and closed minded and absolutistic in saying "men are nothing but apes". You don't know all men. Or suppose you mean that sentence literally. Men—humans—are just animals. Well, you can know that they *are* animals, because there's evidence for that, but you can't know that they're nothing more. They may have souls, things that don't appear on your scientific instruments. So you're claiming a complete knowledge of your subject that you can't have, unless you're God. That's a very unscientific claim.

Libby: Especially if there is no God.

'Isa: But you can't know that, for the same reason: the structure of a universal negative proposition. To know that there is no God anywhere in reality, you'd have to know all reality—and you can do that only if you're God!

Libby: So to know there's no God you have to be God.

'Isa: Yep.

Libby: So you've refuted atheism by formal logic alone. A kind of ontological argument.

'Isa: I'm not claiming that. All I'm claiming is that reductionism is self-contradictory.

Libby: And this is connected to moral relativism . . . how?

'Isa: Reductionism says that morality is nothing but biological survival, the survival of the fittest, natural selection. But to know that, to know that there is in all reality no more-than-biological-survival morality, you have to know all reality.

Libby: Huh! Do you have anything a little less abstract, anything more practical? Ordinary people like myself, as distinct from philosophers, are a little suspicious of formal logic.

'Isa: That doesn't change the laws of logic, you know. Whether you like it or not, a self-contradiction is a self-contradiction. But here— here's a practical refutation of reductionism. It's inhuman. It's "dreary, stale, flat, and unprofitable". And it makes whoever believes it dreary, stale, flat, and unprofitable in thought and in life. It's destructive of human happiness, of hope, of wisdom, of morality, even of survival.

Libby: Well, well, the prophet has quite a list of dooms and damns there. Could you explain to this sceptic, and many others, that last doom? Why is reductionism destructive of *survival*?

'Isa: Because of the principle of "first and second things", as C. S. Lewis calls it.

Libby: What's that?

'Isa: That's the principle that when second things are put first, not only first things but second things too are lost. More exactly, when there are greater goods and lesser goods, or ultimate ends and proximate ends, if we put lesser goods, like survival, before greater goods, like values to survive *for*, then we lose not only the greater goods, the values, but even the lesser good that we've idolized . . .

Libby: And the practical application is . . .

'Isa: That the society that believes in nothing worth surviving for beyond mere survival will not survive.

Libby: Well, let me play the philosopher to the prophet for a minute, if I may. Even if you're right, and reductionism is destructive, the fact that an idea is destructive doesn't prove it's *false*.

'Isa: That's true. But if there's no compelling proof that the idea is true, the realization that the idea will make me unhappy, wicked, shallow, despairing, or dead is a very good reason for not believing it!

Libby: I've got to admit, that's a pretty practical principle. But you haven't proved that reductionism will do that.

'Isa: What kind of proof do you want?

Libby: Something empirical, not just logical.

'Isa: Well, there's no absolute certainty about what will happen empirically, until it happens, of course. But there's powerful probability.

So far, throughout all known human history no society that embraced your philosophy—modernity's philosophy, relativism and reductionism—has survived very long. Here, let me sort out the premises of the argument: reductionism leads to moral relativism. All societies that have survived fairly well so far in history—fairly well in quantity of time and in quality of life—*all* such societies have believed in some absolute morality. Reductionism eliminates any absolute morality. Therefore reductionism very probably eliminates the society that believes it.

Libby: As you say, we have to wait and see to be sure. Meanwhile, we seem to be surviving here rather well.

'Isa: Ah, but you forget this is an island. An island of beauty and fun in a dying world. A temporary vacation spot. An unreal place. A parable of modern society.

Libby: Nuts. I thought I could live on the beach forever. Or till I die, whichever comes first.

Interview 9

The Arguments for Moral Absolutism

Libby: Professor, you said this interview that we're doing tonight would be the most important one. Why?

'Isa: That should be obvious.

Libby: Even to the mind of a woman and a journalist, you mean?

'Isa: That's not what I said, and that's not what I thought. If we don't stick to the objective issue—or is that your strategy, diversion?

Libby: Hoo, boy! He blew away my cover!

'Isa: You're right. Today I shall blow away the cover from moral relativism—seven times.

Libby: You did a pretty formidable job of blowing away my arguments, I must admit. (See how nice I can be?)

'Isa: But just refuting all the *arguments* for relativism doesn't refute relativism, of course. It might still be true, but not provable. (See how fair and logical *I* can be?)

Libby: And that seems to be a very reasonable position to most people, I think—that it's not provable or disprovable. In the absence of proof, it's a personal choice.

'Isa: And that is your position, is it?

Libby: Yes.

'Isa: So moral relativism is based on faith rather than reason, something like religion rather than science?

Libby: No, it's not based on either.

'Isa: On what, then? On feelings and desires? Perhaps the desire to do some of the things moral absolutism forbids?

Libby: I thought we were supposed to be doing logical arguments for absolutism today instead of getting off into amateur psychoanalysis.

'Isa: That's right.

Libby: Then could you please summarize your arguments, one by one?

'Isa: I'll be very happy to. I thought you'd never ask. Here's my list . . . let's see . . . I call them the argument from consequences, the argument from consensus, the argument from experience, the argument from moral argument, the argument from moral language, the logical self-contradiction argument, and the practical self-contradiction argument.

Libby: Is there any particular order to your listing?

'Isa: Yes. They go from weaker to stronger.

Libby: Oh, so not all are equally valid?

'Isa: I think all of them are valid, but they get stronger and more irrefutable as we go along—although not everyone would agree with that ranking, I think, because they also tend to get more and more abstract as they go along, based less on experience and more on formal logic.

Libby: Well, let's hear the first one. That should be the least abstract one, then?

'Isa: Yes. That's the argument from consequences, or the pragmatic argument. It takes off from one of your arguments for relativism. You argued that absolutism was wrong because it had bad consequences, namely intolerance. My quarrel with that argument was *not* with your principle that consequences are at least a relevant indicator, a clue, but only with your other premise that relativism led to tolerance and absolutism to intolerance. I think it's just the opposite: absolutism grounds tolerance much better than relativism. But I accept the principle that "ideas have consequences" and that we should evaluate ideas by their practical consequences as well as by their theoretical soundness, the logic and evidence.

Libby: Sounds good to me so far.

'Isa: Well, then, what would you say is the obvious consequence of moral relativism?

Libby: Tolerance. Something you absolutists have never really understood. Oh, I know you pay lip service to it, but you don't really understand it; you don't see its moral priority. You don't understand where we're coming from.

'Isa: On the contrary, I think absolutists understand that better than relativists do—where you're coming from, I mean. I think Chesterton let that cat out of the bag when he said that tolerance is the one value you have left when you've lost all your principles. If you want to do bad things, you tolerate them in others so that at least you're not a hypocrite.

Libby: Now *you're* not being logical. You're confusing a *consequence* with a *motive*. You're doing amateur psychologizing again.

'Isa: Then let me give you the consequence instead of the motive. Do you want to know what I think is the consequence of relativism?

Libby: What?

'Isa: Tolerance.

Libby: You *agree* with me now?

'Isa: No. I mean tolerance of evil, not tolerance of opinions or persons.

Libby: Oh. The "love the sin, hate the sinner" principle?

'Isa: I think you mean "love the sinner, hate the sin".

Libby: Oh, [expletive deleted], I got it backwards. I guess you're gonna psychoanalyze me on that one now, huh? I know, I got it backwards because I'm the media, right? OK, so seriously now, so your point about consequences is . . . what? It's not perfectly clear to me.

'Isa: Is that because you're the media? It's perfectly clear to everybody else.

Libby: What is?

'Isa: That the consequence of moral relativism is the removal of deterrence. That just as the consequences of moral absolutism, the consequences of "do the right thing" are—doing the right thing; so the consequences of moral relativism, the consequences of "if it feels good, do it" are—doing whatever feels good. It doesn't take a philosopher to see *that*. In fact, it takes a philosopher to *miss* it.

Libby: Thanks for the lefthanded compliment. You never called me a philosopher before.

'Isa: It's a serious point. Isn't it obvious? *All* evil deeds feel good; that's why we do them! If sin didn't feel like fun, we'd all be saints!

Libby: So absolutism makes saints and relativism makes sinners? That's your argument?

'Isa: Yes!

Libby: But a lot of sinners have been absolutists.

'Isa: Yes, but not a single saint has ever been a moral relativist.

Libby: Oh . . .

'Isa: And the same goes for societies. No saintly society has ever been based on moral relativism. Just compare societies founded on the principles of moral relativists like Mussolini and Mao with societies founded on the principles of moral absolutists like Moses and Muhammad. Compare them in their *quantity* of life as well as their *quality* of life; I mean their longevity as well as their stability and peace and happiness.

Libby: But we haven't seen many societies yet that believe in moral relativism. It's a fairly new idea.

'Isa: We've seen enough! Those that we *have* seen in this century have all been murderous, lying, and horrible. And short lived.

Libby: Are you saying America is horrible?

'Isa: Not yet.

Libby: Are you basing your argument on a prophecy now?

'Isa: Not as a premise. But the conclusion is a kind of prophecy, a warning.

Libby: And what is that warning, O prophet? Would you like me to alert the media?

'Isa: That quotation from Mussolini that so rightly bothered you the first day—that'll do. And yes, I'd love you to alert the media—can you do miracles?

Libby: I'm sure you would. Do you plan to send out thousands of copies of the book Professor Kreeft is going to make from these tapes?

'Isa: No, that's the publisher's job. Our job is just to look at the arguments. So can we do our job now? Let's go to my second argument now, if you have no more questions about the first one.

Libby: I'm not clear what kind of questions I'm supposed to be asking. Am I your debate opponent or just your interviewer today—or somewhere in between? I didn't prepare any objections to your arguments, because I haven't even heard them yet.

Kreeft: Do whatever comes naturally, Libby. Ask both kinds of questions if you like. It's not a formal debate. It's an informal interview that's supposed to be spontaneous.

Libby: OK, let's play it by ear. What's your second argument?

'Isa: That's the argument from consensus, or "common consent", as it's been called. It's very simple: nearly everyone who has ever lived has been a moral absolutist. To be a relativist you have to be a snob, because you have to believe that nearly all of the human beings who have ever lived in this world, especially the greatest sages and saints and prophets—they have all based their lives on an illusion, a fantasy, a myth. You have to believe that "we are the people, and wisdom was born with us". Relativists are a tiny minority, almost totally concentrated in one civilization, the modern West.

Libby: Could you define "the modern West"—sociologically, I mean, not just theologically?

'Isa: I mean white, democratic, industrialized, urbanized, secularized, university-educated society. That would be the sociological description. "Apostate Christendom" would be the theological definition.

Libby: So your argument is that forty million Frenchmen *can* be wrong, and so can two hundred million Americans, but two billion savages can't? Are you telling the truth by counting noses now?

'Isa: No. It's only a probable argument. But it should appeal to egalitarians like you, who argue against absolutism because you say it's connected with snobbery. It's exactly the opposite. Absolutism is *traditional* morality, and tradition can be defined as . . .

Libby: I know. You like to quote Chesterton. "The democracy of the dead."

'Isa: The extension of egalitarianism to the past. Chesterton called it the extension of the franchise to vote—extending it to the most powerless of all classes: people who are disenfranchised not "by accident of birth" but by accident of death. Tradition counters the small and arrogant oligarchy of the living, the lucky few who just happen to be walking around.

Libby: You know your Chesterton, anyway. That's almost word for word.

'Isa: You too? I'm surprised you read such old-fashioned moral absolutists.

Libby: For style, not for content. So you think America is—let's see, let's count up the indictments: not traditional, and therefore not really egalitarian, and not absolutist but relativist, and therefore not going to survive very long.

'Isa: It's not going to survive *if* the relativists win over the absolutists.

[Note: Sound communicates more than print. The tape says: "*win-over*", not "*win* over"—"convert", not "beat". The same is true of Libby's response.]

Libby: Oh, I don't think you have to worry about that. People like me are not going to win over people like you.

'Isa: People like me?

Libby: Stubborn dinosaurs, I mean.

'Isa: You think that's the typical profile of the absolutist, don't you?

Libby: Absolutely.

'Isa: So you think we're a minority?

Libby: Of course you are.

'Isa: In your circles, maybe. But not once you get out of the cities and the power elites.

Libby: What's the point? Merely that a poll would show 51% still in favor of absolutism?

'Isa: No, it's more complex than that.

Libby: More philosophically complex?

'Isa: No, more sociologically complex. Even in societies like America where the educators are relativists and almost everybody is overeducated, popular opinion still is absolutist. One sociologist called America "a nation of Indians ruled by an elite of Swedes"—India being the most religious country in the world and Sweden the least.

Libby: There's some racist insult hidden there, I'm sure.

'Isa: The point isn't race; it's ideology. You relativists are like the Communists: you always pretend to be the party of the people, while you really scorn and despise the people's philosophy.

Libby: It sounds like sour grapes to me. You're complaining because we're winning.

'Isa: No, I'm complaining because you're lying. For a whole generation now you small minority of relativistic elitists who somehow gained control of the media have been relentlessly imposing your elitist relativism on popular opinion by accusing popular opinion—I mean traditional morality—of elitism, and of imposing *their* morality! It's like the Nazi propaganda saying Germany was victimized by Poland.

Libby: How hard it is for the philosophy professor to keep to the high road of logic instead of crawling around in the mud of personal insults! Notice, please, that it is I who want to climb back into the clean air of the logic of your argument.

'Isa: Hmph!

Libby: Or do you want to argue about "who started it"? The invective, I mean.

'Isa: I want to argue about what's true.

Libby: And yet you give me an argument based on subjective opinions—on whether there are more people who have absolutist opinions than relativist opinions.

'Isa: As I said, that argument can be only probable. Because it's an argument from authority, the authority of numbers.

Libby: Ah, now you're making sense. If you accept that principle, you're getting modern and scientific instead of arguing from authority.

'Isa: No, I'm getting *medieval* and scientific. "The argument from (human) authority is the weakest of all arguments"—that was a maxim of medieval philosophers.

Libby: What? It sounds like a maxim *against* medieval philosophers.

'Isa: And that historical ignorance of yours shows how successful the modern propaganda has been.

Libby: What historical ignorance? What propaganda?

'Isa: The fact that most people today are as surprised as you are to learn that that maxim about authority was medieval, not modern. You're surprised to hear that because you've been taught that the Middle Ages were authoritarian because they were religious, and that modern, "Enlightenment" civilization is rational because it's secular. But the truth is almost exactly the opposite. Medieval philosophers and theologians of all religious traditions—Jewish, Christian, and Muslim—were rational to a fault, while most modern philosophies since the "Enlightenment" have attacked reason in a dozen different ways and exalted authority instead—the authority of ideology, or politics, or the passions, or power, or pragmatism, or positivism, or Deconstructionism, or Marxism, or Freudianism, or Romanticism, or Existentialism—almost the whole of Western philosophy for the last two centuries has been an attack on reason.

Libby: If we argue about history we'll be here all day. How about if we try to stick to the logic of each argument?

'Isa: Excellent. Let's try. My third argument, then—OK, are we ready to go on?—good. My third argument is the one I already presented the other day: the argument from the data, from moral experience. So we don't have to go over that again. But a fourth one is closely connected with it. I mentioned it the other day as *part* of our moral experience: our experience of how we use moral language. Let me just give a slightly different spin to that argument now, if I may.

Libby: OK.

'Isa: C. S. Lewis uses it very simply and effectively at the beginning of *Mere Christianity*. It's based on the observation that we all have moral arguments, even relativists. We quarrel, we don't just fight, like animals . . .

Libby: How is that supposed to prove there's an absolute morality?

'Isa: It shows that we *believe* there is.

Libby: How does it show that? Why couldn't the quarrel be about our moral feelings?

'Isa: Because we don't *argue* about feelings; we only fight. If only subjective feelings were involved, it would just be a contest of strength between competing feelings. If I'm both hungry and tired, I'll eat if I'm more hungry, and I'll sleep if I'm more tired. But we say things like, "Hey, that isn't fair!" and "What right do you have to take that?" If relativism were true, moral argument would be impossible; it would be arguing about feelings. "You're wrong!" "No, I'm right!" would mean only "I feel lousy about that!" "No, I feel fine about it!" Like "I feel hot!" "But I feel cold!"—with no objective thermometer to tell the real temperature.

Let's just look at the structure of moral argument. It always takes the same form: first, the appeal to some universal moral principle, like "thou shalt not murder", "don't kill innocent people", and then bringing in some factual situation, showing how that principle applies to the situation, like "babies are innocent people", and then drawing the conclusion of the moral syllogism: "Therefore don't kill babies." There's a major premise and a minor premise. The major premise is always some universal moral principle, the minor premise is some particular factual situation, and the conclusion comes from applying the principle to the situation. The *situation* may be particular, but the *principle* has to be universal—so that it can apply to both parties equally. And it has to be objective, for the same reason, and also unchanging, like math, so you can measure with it, so the rules don't change in the middle of the game. For the same reason: to be fair.

Libby: So what's your point?

'Isa: That we all admit the validity of moral argument, the meaningfulness of moral argument in practice, because we *do* it; and that the essential structure of moral argument shows the need for a universal, objective, unchanging principle. Without that principle, without the major premise, you can't have any moral argument at all.

Libby: And you think this analysis of logic proves moral absolutism is true?

'Isa: It proves that either moral absolutism is true or that all moral argument is impossible and meaningless. But moral argument is possible, because it's actual, and it's meaningful. We do it. It works. Therefore . . .

Libby: OK, I can draw the logical conclusion.

'Isa: Well, why don't you, then?

Libby: What do you mean?

'Isa: Why don't you believe what the argument has just proved?

Libby: Because it's *your* argument, not mine, remember?

'Isa: No, no; arguments are not private property, like warts. They're public proofs, like science. And if the premises are true and there's no logical fallacy, then the conclusion has been proved. That's what logic is.

Libby: I understand what logic is.

'Isa: Do you? I wonder. Tell me, if the conclusion has been proved, what has it been proved to be?

Libby: What?

'Isa: That's my question, "What?" Proved to be *what*?

Libby: Proved to be true.

'Isa: And if a conclusion is proved to be true, really proved to be true, validly proved to be true, then it *is* true!

Libby: But not everything true can be proved to be true.

'Isa: No, but everything proved to be true is true.

Libby: OK. So? What's the point of your lesson in elementary logic?

'Isa: So if it's true, why don't you believe it?

Libby: Why don't I believe your conclusion? Because your conclusion is absolutism, and I'm a relativist, not an absolutist. Or hadn't you noticed?

'Isa: But you've just been shown that absolutism is true. Don't you want to believe the truth?

Libby: Not if it's your kind of truth.

'Isa: Libby, sometimes you're just impossible.

Libby: Why thank you, Professor! Can we get to the next argument now?

'Isa: I don't know if we should. It's not illogical enough for you. In fact, it's so totally logical that it's based on only one premise, which is the fundamental law of all logic, the law of noncontradiction. That's why I call it the self-contradiction argument. I say that relativistic morality is not only *bad* and not only *false*; it's self-contradictory. "Relativistic morality" is like "illogical logic". It's oxymoronic.

Libby: Are you sure you don't want to just drop the "oxy" and say "moronic"? Personal insult is more your style, isn't it?

'Isa: My point is that the alternative to absolute morality is not some other kind of morality, any other kind of morality—because there *is* no other kind of morality—but no morality at all, just feelings, or conventions, or consensus, or games, or social approval. The whole moral *dimension* is missing. So when you say "absolute morality", you say something like "three-sided triangle." If it isn't three sided, it isn't a triangle.

Libby: Why can't morality be gentle instead of hard? Free ideals instead of impositions? Wise suggestions?

'Isa: Suggestions! Moral obligations aren't *suggestions*; they're *commands*. Moses didn't give the Jews God's Ten Suggestions, or Ten Ideals, or God's Top Ten Values.

Libby: So you're arguing that absolutism is inherent in the very essence of morality.

'Isa: Yes.

Libby: As existence is in the very essence of God? That's Anselm's "ontological argument", isn't it?

'**Isa:** In a sense, yes; the structure is parallel. Perhaps we should state that argument for the tape.

Libby: I can do that. Let's see . . . The argument says that God must exist because existence is a perfection, and every perfection must be in the very essence of God because God by definition is the most perfect being, the being that has all possible perfections, therefore God must exist. Right? Anselm tried to prove atheism was logically self-contradictory, and you're trying the same logic on relativism, aren't you?

'**Isa:** Yes. That's very good, Libby. By the way, I don't think Anselm's argument proves God, but I do think my argument proves absolutism.

Libby: Why? What's the difference?

'**Isa:** Because Anselm's argument has a hidden assumption that's false: it assumes that we can know God's essence. But we *can* know the essence of human morality.

Libby: Oh. Well, your argument is awfully abstract, anyway—in *that* way it's like Anselm's argument. So I don't think many people are going to be swayed by it. But I don't know how else to logically critique it—you're the philosophy professor—so let's go on to your next argument.

'**Isa:** OK. This is the last one, the practical self-contradiction argument or the ad hominem argument. Its premise is the actual practice of the relativist. The last argument found a self-contradiction in the idea itself, in the theory; this argument finds a self-contradiction in the relativist's practice.

Libby: What practice?

'**Isa:** The fact that relativists act like absolutists when you do *them* an injustice. They say, "No fair!" just like everybody else. They don't just say, "I feel very bad about that"—unless they've lost their humanity and their sanity and exchanged them for psychology.

Libby: "Unless they've lost their humanity and their sanity and exchanged them for psychology"—that's supposed to be a logical argument? Hey, Mister Logic Professor, ever hear of question-begging rhetoric?

'**Isa:** OK, drop the rhetoric. The point is, they contradict themselves. They say there are no absolute principles to appeal to, but then appeal to them when they say things like "No fair!" And if they don't say things like that . . .

Libby: If they don't, they've lost their humanity. End of discussion. Case closed. Great argument.

'**Isa:** No. If they don't, then there's another contradiction. There's a contradiction in their very act of teaching relativism. Why do relativists teach relativism? Why do they write books? Tell me.

Libby: To emancipate suffering humanity from the oppressive tyranny of absolutists like you.

'**Isa:** Would you like to convince us absolutists that relativism is right and absolutism is wrong?

Libby: Sure.

'**Isa:** Really right and really wrong?

Libby: Yes.

'**Isa:** Then there *is* a real right and wrong. But that's what *absolutism* says.

Libby: All right, no, then. "There is nothing right or wrong, but thinking makes it so."

'**Isa:** Then there's nothing wrong with being an absolutist, and nothing right with being a relativist.

Libby: That's very clever.

'**Isa:** Not at all. No cleverer than the little boy in "The Emperor's New Clothes". It only sees and says the obvious.

Libby: I grant you it's clever, but I don't grant you it's obvious.

'**Isa:** It is once you blow away the smokescreen of your propaganda.

Libby: *You* blow the smoke.

'**Isa:** All I blew was your cover.

Libby: With your superior spiritual powers?

'Isa: No, it's easy. A little boy can do it, like in the fairy tale ["The Emperor's New Clothes"]. All you need is a little logic to see the contradiction between your theory and your practice.

Libby: And this poor woman, of course, can't be expected to have even a little logic!

'Isa: No, it's not *you*—not you as woman or as Libby, but as relativist. You relativists contradict yourselves. You talk about emancipating humanity from the terrible repressions of absolutism, and from all the effort you put into your missionary enterprise, one might have expected that you believed your message was really *true*, and teaching it was really *good*. But your message is that "there is nothing good or bad, but thinking makes it so".

Libby: You call it a "missionary enterprise", but you're the missionaries, you absolutists. You're the preachers.

'Isa: We are. We admit it. You are too, though, but you don't admit it. You relativists preach against preaching. You're on a mission against missionaries. You're missionaries without a religion. You're like the joke about cloning a Jehovah's Witness and a Unitarian together: you get someone who goes door to door with nothing to say.

Libby: Oh, that's a cute little insult to two religions, but it's hardly an argument. Do you have a point hidden there somewhere?

'Isa: The point is: you relativists are Unitarians in theory and Witnesses in practice. That there's a contradiction between your theory and your practice.

Libby: Yeah? Where's the contradiction between believing that there's no absolute truth and not banging people over the head with it? Where's the contradiction between not having any dogma and teaching that you shouldn't have any dogma?

'Isa: Oh, is that your dogma? That you shouldn't have any dogma?

Libby: That's not our dogma. That's our hypothesis.

'Isa: That's not your hypothesis; that's your hypocrisy.

Libby: Oh, I get it now. Here's the bottom line of your terribly objective logical argument, in other words: "Shut your filthy mouth, you dog of an infidel!"

'Isa: Did I say that?

Libby: To me you did.

'Isa: Because I called relativism hypocritical?

Libby: Yeah . . .

'Isa: Hypocrisy—that means means preaching what you don't practice, doesn't it?

Libby: Yeah . . .

'Isa: Well, all I'm saying is either practice what you preach or else preach what you practice. If you practice the relativism you preach, you'll stop preaching. If you preach what you practice, you'll start preaching commonsense morality and a real right and wrong.

Libby: And so, as the moon rises in the sky and the tape runs out, together with my patience, we once again end on the high note of detached scientific logic, pure and disinterested, thus confirming the professor's theory of an absolute, objective, impersonal, and universal truth. Thank you, Professor, for a brilliant performance free from all hypocrisy.

'Isa: How does she *do* that?

Interview 10

The Philosophical
Assumptions of Absolutism

Libby: It sounds strange to be exploring the premises of your argument *after* you think you've proved the conclusion. But that's what we're doing today. Professor, could you please begin by explaining why you thought it necessary to devote a whole interview to the question of the *assumptions* of moral absolutism this morning?

No, wait, let me start over. I want to begin more candidly. I want to confess I have mixed feelings about these interviews so far. I'm disappointed about the objectivity of our interviews—though to be honest with you, I didn't think we could pull that one off, after our past history—but I'm impressed by the fact that you chose to do today's topic, the assumptions of absolutism. Because that's like exposing all your weak points. Because if any of these necessary assumptions is false, absolutism falls too. They are its foundations. So that sounds pretty objective and fair of you. I think you're really *trying* to be objective.

'Isa: It's not just to be fair but to be complete. I think the foundational issues are still ahead of us. And the foundational issues always turn out to be metaphysical. Ethics always rests on metaphysics; what ought to be rests on what is.

Libby: Doesn't it depend on anthropology?

'Isa: That too, of course. Because what we ought to do depends on what we are. If we're only clever apes, then let's ape the apes. If we're gods, let's claim the rights of gods. But anthropology, in turn, depends on metaphysics; what we are depends on what is. If you have a materialist metaphysics, you have a materialist anthropology and a materialist ethics. And ethics also depends on epistemology . . .

Libby: The science of thought.

'Isa: Yes. Because what you think goodness is, and what you think humanity is, and what you think being is, depend on how you think, on what thinking is.

Libby: You'd put it that way rather than the other way round? Epistemology is more fundamental than metaphysics?

'Isa: No; metaphysics has to be fundamental, because what you think depends on what you are.

Libby: What *you* are—human, anthropoid—that's anthropology, not metaphysics.

'Isa: OK, epistemology depends on anthropology, and anthropology depends on metaphysics. What you can think depends on what you are—ape, angel, or something in between—and what you are depends on what is—matter, spirit, both, or neither.

Libby: I think we're getting too technical and abstract for nonphilosophers. Please just tell me what you think are the basic presuppositions of moral absolutism.

'Isa: OK. Let's begin with epistemology. The presupposition here is that we can know truth. In other words, scepticism has to be refuted. Because if scepticism is true, we can't know any truth; and if we can't know any truth, or any timeless truth, or any universal truth, or any objective truth, then we obviously can't know any such truths about morality.

Libby: That makes sense. And do you have a short refutation of scepticism?

'Isa: It'll have to be very short. Establishing these presuppositions took thousands of years of thought, and weakening them took hundreds of years, so shoring them up isn't going to be done in a minute. But essentially, I'd say all forms of scepticism are self-contradictory. Is it true that there is no truth? Is it certain that we can never be certain? Is it an unchangeable truth that there is no unchangeable truth? An objective truth that there is no objective truth? Absolutely true that all truth is relative? Et cetera, et cetera.

Libby: So much for scepticism. Sorry, Socrates.

'Isa: Socrates? He was no sceptic. He was an enemy of the sceptics, the Sophists. *They* were your models; they were the relativists. No, let's not get into all that history again. I just want to repeat one thing I think I said the other day about scepticism: don't confuse scepticism as an attitude, or a method, with scepticism as a philosophy. Socrates was sceptical in temperament, and his method was to question everything. But he believed in absolute truth; he was no sceptic.

Libby: I guess we just have to take your word for that, Professor. Next . . .

'Isa: No you don't. You have to take the word of the data. Read Socrates himself.

Libby: I'm sure that's an excellent idea. Now what's the next premise of absolutism?

'Isa: Another epistemological premise: technically, it's called epistemological realism. Its alternative, epistemological idealism, also has to be refuted.

Libby: Obviously, we need to define our terms.

'Isa: Yes, we do.

Libby: What is epistemological idealism?

'Isa: There are really two forms of it. One is Locke's doctrine that the immediate objects of our knowledge are our own ideas, not objective realities. The other is Kant's doctrine that he called the "Copernican revolution in philosophy": that our ideas determine and form objective reality rather than vice versa.

Libby: OK, why do we have to refute these two ideas?

'Isa: Let's take Locke first. The first sentence in his *Essay on Human Understanding*, or *Treatise on Human Understanding*—I can never remember those dull titles—is that "idea equals object of knowledge". If that's true, if the only things we know at first and immediately are ideas, then morality becomes a set of ideas too.

Libby: What's wrong with that? Of course morality is a set of ideas.

'Isa: No it's not. Knowing moral *ideas* isn't knowing real morality, any more than knowing elvish ideas is knowing real elves.

Libby: You mean idealism reduces morality to a kind of good fantasy?

'**Isa:** Exactly. That's why the words *ideals* and *values* became popular only after Locke and Kant. They're nice, soft, squooshy words. They *feel* subjective.

Libby: What words did they use before?

'**Isa:** Objective words like *good* and *evil* and *virtue* and *vice*. Strong, hard words like *law* and *sin* and *righteousness*. Clear and simple words that you couldn't escape.

Libby: And do you have a logical refutation of Locke, as distinct from a list of favorite adjectives?

'**Isa:** A very short and simple one. If Locke's epistemological idealism is true, if all I immediately know are *ideas*, and everything else is only an inference from them, then I can't be sure which of these ideas I know are *true*, which of them match the reality beyond them, the objective reality that I *don't* know directly but only by inference from my ideas, according to Locke. It's like judging reality from pictures instead of judging pictures by reality. If idealism is true, I'm like a prisoner in a room without windows watching a TV screen all day without ever being allowed to go outside. How do I know which images on the screen correspond to the real outside world?

Libby: You don't.

'**Isa:** Exactly. So epistemological idealism leads to scepticism. Locke leads to Hume.

Libby: I see. And epistemological scepticism leads to moral scepticism.

'**Isa:** Yes. It does, and it did.

Libby: Now what about the second sense of idealism that you mentioned, Kant's "Copernican revolution"? What, exactly, is that, and why do you have to refute that, and *how* do you refute that?

'**Isa:** That's the idea that consciousness structures reality instead of vice versa, that man creates all the form and shape and meaning of the world in the act of knowing it, like an artist instead of a scientist. Professor Kreeft explained it once in class with a haunting image: two men shipwrecked on a desert island find a message in a bottle that washes up on the beach. They read it with hope, and then suddenly the hope changes to despair as they look at the message and say, "It's only from us."

I have to refute that philosophy because if it's true, if our consciousness structures reality rather than reality structuring our consciousness, then the only way to have an absolute moral law, the only way to have a "Categorical Imperative", as Kant called it, is for us to make it, to will it, not to discover it. That's what Kant called "the autonomy of the will". It's the new morality that follows from the new epistemology of "the Copernican revolution".

Libby: Are you saying Kant justified a kind of "do your own thing" morality?

'Isa: No, no, that's not fair. Kant tried to justify moral absolutism. He tried to prove that moral law was both *necessary* and *universal*, even though he denied it was *objective*, denied our ability to know its objective reality, or objective truth. In fact, he denied our ability to know *any* objective reality, or "things in themselves".

Libby: Not objective, but necessary and universal. Hey, two out of three ain't bad, as the song says. Why can't you be happy with that?

'Isa: Because it destroys morality, even though Kant didn't mean to. His intentions were good, but that's not enough. (By the way, that refutes his ethics, because his ethics says good intentions *are* enough.)

Libby: He didn't think it destroyed morality. Why do you?

'Isa: To answer that one, I'm afraid I'm going to have to get a bit technical. Let's look at Kant's "grand strategy". The strategy of his morality in his *Critique of Practical Reason* was parallel to the strategy of his epistemology in *The Critique of Pure Reason*, where he tried to demonstrate the *necessity* and *universality* of the categories of "pure reason" without their *objectivity*. He denied that we could know objective reality, or "things in themselves". But his successors, beginning with Fichte, saw the contradiction there in claiming to know the existence of unknowables. If we can't know objectively real "things in themselves", then we can't know whether there *is* any objective reality, any objectively real things, and everything dissolves into subjectivity. Remember Wittgenstein's line? You quoted it the other day. "To draw a limit to thought, thought must think both sides of that limit." The rational critique of reason is a self-contradiction.

Libby: I follow that. Now how does it apply to *morality*?

'Isa: Just as Kant reduced objective *knowledge* to a kind of necessary dream, a universal dream, he reduced *morality* to a necessary and universal value dream, a "postulate", he called it, a demand of the moral will. The problem is that dreams make no demands on us, even if they're necessary and universal dreams. They can't make demands on us because they come from us. They're "only from us". If we make up moral law, if morality is "autonomous" rather than "heteronomous", as Kant says, then we are our own judge and jury—in fact, our own God. But then I'm not really *under* moral law at all. If I lock myself in a room, but I keep the key, am I really bound? It's like a game.

Libby: I see the problem. And the alternative?

'Isa: The alternative to epistemological idealism is epistemological realism, which is summed up in the maxim the medieval Scholastic philosophers called "the principle of intelligibility": that reality is intelligible to human reason and that human reason is intelligent about reality; that intelligence and intelligibility are open to each other.

Libby: So you have a bridge between knowledge and reality and between epistemology and metaphysics.

'Isa: Yes.

Libby: But isn't that assumption of realism just as much a choice of the will as Kant's alternative, idealism?

'Isa: No, because it doesn't come from our will; it comes from our experience, our data. It's not just from us! It comes *to* us.

Libby: It's a theory, like any other; in that sense it comes from us. It didn't drop down out of the sky.

'Isa: No, but the *theory* of realism is based on the *data*. In fact, it's really only an unfolding of the first certainty we all had as soon as we were born: "There's something there!"

Libby: But how do we know that? How can you prove that?

'Isa: No, that's—

Libby: "No"? "No" is not a grammatical answer to the question "How?"

'Isa: If you'll let me finish, I was trying to say that that's not the first question we ask, or the first question we answer. What *is*? *That's* the first question. First, something is. Then, we know it. Then, we think about how we knew it. You can't know how you know first. You can't know how you know until you know, and you can't know until there's something there to know. So "something's there" has to be first.

Libby: And what does this have to do with moral absolutism?

'Isa: It's the foundation of metaphysics, and metaphysics is the foundation of morality. If you doubt this first certainty, you have no metaphysics. And if you have no metaphysics—if you have no knowledge of truths about objective reality—then of course you have no moral knowledge either, no moral truths.

Libby: I see. So metaphysics is necessary for moral absolutism.

'Isa: I think so. Though not all philosophers would agree with me there.

Libby: Which metaphysics? Will any one do, or do you have to pass some litmus test within metaphysics too?

'Isa: There are some philosophical systems within metaphysics that make moral absolutism impossible too. Nominalism, for instance. If Nominalism is right and there are no real universals, there are no moral universals either. If we can't know any universal truths, then we can't know any universal moral truths either.

Libby: You make it sound so simple.

'Isa: Thank you.

Libby: I didn't mean it as a compliment.

'Isa: You should have.

Libby: Do you have any other metaphysical villains?

'Isa: Many. Obviously, materialism is one. If you're a materialist, if everything is matter, then there's no soul to make moral choices. Atoms aren't moral or immoral, so if everything is only atoms, nothing is really moral. The only *place* for virtues and vices and responsibilities and rights to inhere in is souls, not bodies. Spirit is the only intelligible *locus* for morality.

And here's another one: Determinism, the denial of free will. That's usually a consequence of materialism, since matter has no will; only spirit does. If you're a fatalist, then there's no responsibility. "Que sera, sera." You don't praise or blame a machine, because that's not a moral agent. When the soda machine "steals" your money without giving you your soda, you don't argue with it, or preach at it, or tell it to repent. You kick it. And we don't appeal to animals' free choice either. We *train* them. So if you're a consistent determinist, you kick people—or perhaps you use sweet kicks, sugar kicks, like the treats we use to lure animals. And that's Behaviorism, the psychology of the materialist and the animal trainer.

Libby: Don't you think that's a bit unfair to Behaviorism? Behaviorism emphasizes positive reinforcement, not negative. Strokes, not kicks.

'Isa: Why?

Libby: Works better.

'Isa: But it doesn't. Machiavelli found that out. "Is it better to be feared or to be loved? . . . It is better to be feared, since men love you when they will, but they fear you when you will." Now that's efficiency, if that's all you want.

Libby: All the same, Behaviorism works, "operant conditioning" works—a lot better than preaching sin and guilt.

'Isa: Yes, it does. That's what Hitler discovered. It's much more efficient to treat people like animals or machines. Kick them or lure them; don't preach morality at them. You can believe that if you want, and you can run your society that way if you like, but just don't invite me there, please.

And here's another metaphysical villain: the opposite of materialism and atheism: Pantheism. Atheism says there's no creator; pantheism says there's no creature. Atheism has no God; pantheism has nothing but God. If you're a pantheist, we're all God, so there's no sin.

Libby: And will you now refute all three of those heresies in a sentence or two?

Interview 10: The Philosophical Assumptions of Absolutism / 157

'Isa: I thought I just did. I showed how they destroy morality. So if there is morality, those metaphysics are all wrong.

Libby: Oh. Now you're arguing from morality to metaphysics. I thought you said morality had to be based on metaphysics. Which comes first?

'Isa: We can argue forward or backward—cause to effect or effect to cause.

Libby: So do you think you've killed these thousand-year-old metaphysical dragons in one minute's swinging of your verbal swords today?

'Isa: Of course not. My job today is just to expose some of the dragons, or the termites that eat away the foundations of morality, not to kill them.

Libby: Do you want to mention any more metaphysical termites?

'Isa: One more, anyway: Cartesian dualism. The simple, strict separation of matter and spirit. Matter is out there, and takes up space, and doesn't think. Spirit is in here, and doesn't take up space, and thinks. And those are the two kinds of reality, according to Descartes. I think most people in our society are Cartesians. That's how we think of matter and spirit. That's our common sense, as Aristotle's hylomorphism was Greek common sense. Aristotle married what Descartes divorced.

Libby: And how does this Cartesian dualism eliminate morality?

'Isa: If what's out there is only matter and energy, and spirit exists only inside human souls, then there's no place for an objective natural law, an objective moral law. What's "out there" has to be more than matter if morality is going to be "out there", or objective.

Libby: So is that it for your metaphysical hit list?

'Isa: I think that's it. But there are also some essential presuppositions of morality in anthropology, or philosophical psychology, or philosophy of human nature. (It used to be called "philosophy of man", until you feminists told us "man" didn't mean what everybody thought it meant for centuries.) One of the most controversial ideas today is simply that human nature exists. Nominalists of all kinds deny that and Marxists, and racists, new or old. Nominalists can't talk about any universal natures, including human nature.

Libby: Nominalists seem to be in the forefront of your hit list.

'Isa: I think a lot of the current confusion in morality stems from Nominalism in anthropology, and the fear of the N word: *natural*, and its opposite, *unnatural*.

Libby: Why do you say that?

'Isa: Think about it: Who talks about "unnatural acts" any more?

Libby: Fundamentalists like you.

'Isa: I'll ignore that. So once you lose the concept of what's natural, what's in accordance with human nature, you reduce the *natural* to the *common*, the statistically common, the empirically verifiable. Quantity replaces quality. Whatever is socially accepted now becomes normative.

Libby: That's what *normative means*.

'Isa: Only to a sociologist.

Libby: You say that word like a curse.

'Isa: I should be more specific: a sociologist ignorant of the distinction between *nomos* and *logos*, between ethos and ethics.

Libby: Somehow I feel a sermon coming on.

'Isa: I hope you're noticing how well I'm resisting your temptations to descend from debate to mudslinging.

Libby: I'm amazed. What's come over you today?

'Isa: The point is just too important. The whole moral dimension is sliding away into ignorance today, and you don't realize it. It's like a whole society going color blind and thinking black and white are the only colors anyone ever saw.

Libby: That does sound serious. But it also sounds like Chicken Little.

'Isa: Let me give you some examples. Practices like sodomy and contraception and fornication are common today and, more important, commonly *accepted* in the same way as different styles of food or clothing. Nobody calls them "unnatural acts". But until the sixties, everybody did.

Libby: Things change.

'Isa: Opinions change, but essences don't.

Libby: Life changes. Lifestyles change.

'Isa: But the badness of acts contrary to human nature doesn't change, because that's not from opinions or fashions but from their nature, their essence, which doesn't change, and from human nature, which doesn't change. They're not in accord with human nature and the natural ends and purposes of man and woman and marriage and sex and fertility.

Libby: So it's only about sex?

'Isa: Let me give you an example that isn't. Take death. A "natural death" is a traditional concept that many intelligent people somehow find just unintelligible any more. So the distinction between killing and letting die, between Kevorkianizing a cancer patient and just not giving any more chemotherapy—people think that's a hairsplitting distinction today. We're losing the concept of a natural death just as we're losing the concept of a natural life.

Libby: But don't you think that's because of the progress of technology, life-extending technologies? The line just isn't clear any more between the so-called natural means or ordinary means of sustaining life and so-called unnatural means or extraordinary means. A respirator or a dialysis machine was once considered extraordinary. Even penicillin was extraordinary in 1940.

'Isa: That's part of it, I grant you. But a much bigger part is the decline in the understanding of the very concept of what's natural.

Libby: And that comes from Nominalism, and leads to Armageddon —is that what you say?

'Isa: I'll say that, yes.

Libby: So say you. But almost nobody else. So it's Catholics and Muslims against the world.

'Isa: But that makes almost three billion—almost half the world. And if you add our allies who have not bowed the knee to Baal—Orthodox Jews and Eastern Orthodox Christians, and Evangelicals, and Mormons—and Confucians and Buddhists and some Hindus—that's not an extremist fringe, though you media people always call us "right-wing religious fundamentalists".

Libby: Are you saying it's about religion?

'Isa: It's not about one religion; it's about the religious philosophy of life.

Libby: Ah, now we get to the real presupposition of absolutism. It is a religious issue after all, not a philosophical issue. Moral absolutism comes from religious absolutism, religious fundamentalism. It's really that simple.

'Isa: It is *not* really that simple. For one thing, absolutism and fundamentalism aren't the same thing at all.

Libby: Look, I'm going to be pushy here. I don't want to define any more isms. Just tell me this: What more are you saying than Dostoyevski said: "If there is no God, everything is permissible"?

'Isa: The relation between religion and morality isn't as simple as that.

Libby: Why not?

'Isa: For one thing, because even atheists can be moral absolutists.

Libby: How is that possible? Is God just an extra, then? I thought you religious people thought God was the ultimate source of morality. Don't you believe that?

'Isa: Yes, but even though God is in fact the real source of morality, our *knowledge* of God is not the only source of our knowledge of morality.

Libby: Could you explain that, please?

'Isa: In objective fact, it's God's will—or God's character—that is the First Cause of the moral law. But in our subjective consciousness, we don't have to *know* the First Cause before we know second causes. It's like science. What's true in science is also true in morality: you can know the second cause without knowing the first cause. You can be an atheist and still be a good scientist, even though God is in fact the First Cause of everything you know because he created the universe. So you can also know a lot about the moral second causes, or the moral effects, without knowing their ultimate cause.

Libby: So religion isn't really necessary for morality, then.

'Isa: Practically speaking, it is. You get a very few agnostics who are morally wise, but not many. And that's just what you'd expect if we're fallen and sinful and stupid creatures, isn't it? A direct revelation from God, the pure source of moral goodness, would be like the sun, and our fallen human minds' understanding of morality on their own, without God, would be like a flashlight.

Libby: *If* we're so fallen and sinful as you say. But that view depends on religious faith.

'Isa: No it doesn't. What is it Chesterton said?—sin is the only dogma of religion that can be proved just by reading the newspapers.

Libby: I see your point. I believe Hegel called history a slaughter bench.

'Isa: And throughout history, religion has always been the firmest support for morality.

Libby: That's because past societies usually co-opted some religious orthodoxy for their social order. The separation of church and state is a pretty new idea.

'Isa: But even in a secular society like America it's still true that religion is the firmest support for morality. There has never been a popular secular morality that's lasted and worked in holding a society together. Society has always needed morality, and morality has always needed religion. Destroy religion, you destroy morality; destroy morality, you destroy society. That's history's bottom line.

Libby: And yours too? Shall we conclude this interview on that prophetic note?

'Isa: Yes, let's. And the reminder that "those who do not learn from history are condemned to repeat it".

Kreeft: *And* the reminder that the sun is out and the surf is up. It's going to be four to six feet this afternoon. High tide is at six thirty something; why not finish the last interview right now so we can have the whole rest of the day to go to heaven?

Libby: Great. I can hold off lunch, what about you?

'Isa: Let's go for it.

Interview 11

The Cause and Cure of Relativism

Libby: OK. Professor, you wanted this last interview to be about "the cause and cure of moral relativism." I want to begin by pointing out the obvious: that the word *cure assumes* that moral relativism is some kind of disease.

'Isa: No.

Libby: No, it's *not* a disease?

'Isa: No, I'm not assuming that. I've proved it. So it's not an assumption; it's a conclusion. What we're doing today is the practical corollary. We've proved it's wrong, so now we want to know how to cure it; and to know *that*, we have to know what *causes* it.

Libby: The cause and cure go together, I take it? Kind of two halves of the same coin?

'Isa: Yes. For instance, one of the causes of moral relativism, I think, is the loss of the four cardinal virtues, so one of its cures would be the restoration of them. In both theory and practice, I mean. You no longer *know* the four cardinal virtues, you no longer believe in them, and therefore you also no longer practice them, or even try to.

Libby: "You"? Who is this "you"?

'Isa: Modern society, secular society, apostate society . . .

Libby: OK, OK, we've been through that. So give us the four cardinal virtues.

'Isa: They're really just one thing with three aspects or parts . . .

Libby: Like the Trinity?

'Isa: Perhaps. Don't Christians believe in one God yet at the same time three . . . well, they say it's not three parts but three *Persons*, don't they? You tell me; you're a Christian, aren't you?

Libby: Well, sort of.

'Isa: What kind of an answer is that?

Libby: I never really understood it all, so I guess I never really believed it. The doctrines, I mean.

'Isa: That too?

Libby: "Too"?

'Isa: It seems to me it's the morality that you've most definitively left behind. So what's the "sort of" that's left? The liturgy?

Libby: No, I don't go to church.

'Isa: So what do you mean saying you're some kind of Christian?

Libby: I don't know. Maybe I'm not. Who knows?

'Isa: *You* don't, that's for sure. Anyway, the four cardinal virtues are a kind of trinity, or trunity: one thing with three aspects, or three *somethings*—in Plato's version, anyway. The three parts are wisdom, courage, and self-control, and together they make up justice. Wisdom means knowing the truth, especially the moral truth, the truth about the good to be done. Courage means the will choosing the good even when it hurts, the will following the reason instead of the desires when reason says X is good and the desires say X doesn't feel good, when it gives pain instead of pleasure. And self-control means not following passion when passion says X is fun and reason says it's evil—not listening to the philosophy that says, "It can't be wrong if it feels so right." It's also called temperance: tempering the feelings or desires, controlling the desires, moderating them, not being a fanatic about any one, like alcohol or money or media approval—or sex.

Libby: And you think these four cardinal virtues have just—sort of *died*? Like Nietzsche's "God is dead"?

'Isa: In the minds of your society's mind molders, yes. Especially self-control, because I think that's the least popular of all the virtues in your society, the one that has a really bad press. The psychologists give it nasty names like "repression". But it's almost the essence of civilization. Plato noted that it wasn't just one of the cardinal virtues but a necessary ingredient in all virtues. If you trash it, as you've done, you get trashed. If you lose it in your individual life, your life comes apart. If you lose it in your social life, your social life comes apart.

Libby: Why?

'Isa: Because if reason doesn't rule passion, passion will rule reason, and then reason becomes rationalization—rationalization of your passions, a slave of your passions—propaganda, advertising.

Libby: So you want to hear three cheers for repression.

'Isa: No, for self-control. That's not the same thing as repression, any more than taming a wild horse and riding it is the same as tying it up in the barn. It's order; it's hierarchy; it's governing.

Libby: Look, Professor, we're Americans here. We don't go for hierarchy. We don't do kings.

'Isa: Too bad for you.

Libby: You're bad-mouthing democracy now?

'Isa: Not in society. Your society might work without a king, but your soul won't. Because if you have no king within, you have no order.

Libby: Equality is our order.

'Isa: So every desire gets an equal vote? A perfect recipe for chaos.

Libby: So you say Plato was right that reason should be the king of the soul?

'Isa: Yes.

Libby: So you think we ought to do everything by the book? Before we fall in love we should stop and check our syllogisms for fallacies?

'Isa: No. Reason doesn't mean just logic. But I do think it would be an excellent idea if we *thought* about it before falling in love with the wrong person. You think before you join the army, or a political party, or a church; why not before you join a relationship?

Libby: So love should bow to logic.

'Isa: I just told you I don't mean just logic. Reason, intelligence, insight, wisdom—light. You're substituting heat for light.

Libby: Nice idea, Plato, but it's a little outdated. Haven't you heard the news? Love is blind.

'Isa: No it isn't. Lust is blind. That's why it confuses itself with love.

Libby: Aha, now we come to the root of the matter. We've finally found the principle that preserves civilization: sexual repression. Do you realize how perfectly you confirm what Freud said?

'Isa: Freud was right about one thing, at least: sexual passion is the strongest and most attractive of all the passions, maybe even stronger than the instinct for self-preservation. Though it hardly took Freud to discover that! So it follows that it's the most addictive. And the most blinding. Addicts can't think clearly. Their drug scrambles their brains, and the desire for their drug scrambles their souls.

Libby: Ooh, I've been diagnosed with scrambled soul now! Is that edible? Look, Professor, seriously, there's a communications gap here. You live in another world. You haven't heard the news: there's been a revolution. It's called the sexual revolution. Like it or not, we're postrevolutionaries.

'Isa: That's my point, exactly. What could be more revolutionary than a revolution that changes how we look at the very origin of life itself?

Libby: What do you mean?

'Isa: Haven't *you* heard the news? It's the *sexual* revolution.

Libby: Yeah, so?

'Isa: What do you think the origin of life is? The stork?

Libby: Oh. But that's under our control now. That's the revolution. It doesn't *have* to be the origin of life any more. There's this pill, you see . . . or perhaps you haven't heard *that* news?

'Isa: You're proving my point with every word you say. I absolutely agree with you: Dr. Rock's pill sparked one of the most revolutionary revolutions in history. It separated sex from its essence—the origin of life—and reduced it to its accident—fun. And now you look at its essence as an "accident" to be "controlled" and prevented!

Libby: You sound like the Pope.

'Isa: I don't deserve that compliment, but thank you anyway.

Libby: So you see the sexual revolution as something satanic?

'Isa: I'm no expert in demonology, but I can't imagine a more effective satanic strategy for undermining our moral knowledge and our moral life than the sexual revolution.

Libby: You have the prophet's talent for being incendiary, I'll give you that.

'Isa: No, look at the hard evidence. Already the new demand for sexual "freedom" has conquered one of the strongest instincts in human history.

Libby: You mean morality?

'Isa: No. Morality's not an *instinct*. I mean motherhood. A million American mothers a year now abort their children—and their motherhood. They pay hired killers called doctors to kill their own sons and daughters before they can be born. Nobody in the world thought that could ever happen before the sexual revolution. The only reason it can happen is the sexual revolution. Your abortion holocaust comes from the sexual revolution just as certainly as the Nazis' Holocaust came from their racist revolution.

Libby: You're foaming at the mouth, Professor.

'Isa: No, I'm coldly analyzing an obsession. I'm dissecting a corpse.

Libby: You're saying abortion is all about sex.

'Isa: Of course!

Libby: Prove it.

'Isa: That's obvious. Why does anyone want an abortion? Abortion means backup birth control, right?

Libby: Yeah . . .

'Isa: And what is birth control? Birth control means the demand to have sex without having babies, right?

Libby: Well . . .

'Isa: If babies came from having a stork instead of having sex, how much abortion do you think there would be?

Libby: And you say this is "hard evidence" for some sort of social sexual pathology?

'Isa: Horribly hard! And here's another piece of hard evidence. Imagine this scenario, please. Suppose half of all the children in America chose to commit suicide. Wouldn't that be hard evidence of a social disaster?

Libby: Of course. But that's not happening.

'Isa: Something like it is. Half of all your marriages end in divorce. And that's suicide—the suicide of the new joint person created by the marriage, when the two become "one flesh". Remember? "They are now no longer two, but one." That's what you deliberately try to kill when you divorce. It's the same kind of murderous violence as abortion.

Libby: That's really incendiary language. I thought you were all in favor of reason and logic.

'Isa: That *is* reason and logic. You're the ones who are obsessed with passion, and it makes you blind to the logic. Look here, just try to look at the issue reasonably for one minute . . .

Libby: With that kind of insult as an invitation, who could refuse?

'Isa: Suppose there was some other practice, not divorce, and not connected to sex in any way—let's call it X—that had three results. First of all, it betrayed the person you promised never to betray; it broke the most solemn promise you ever made in your life, your promise to that person you claimed to love more than anything else. It deliberately lied to him, cheated on him, threw him away like garbage, after you said to him, "Trust me, come to me, I will never abandon you." Second, suppose X also betrayed your children, broke your promise of security to them, scarred them for life—the vulnerable little ones that you procreated, that you are responsible for, that you promised to protect. Suppose it hurt them more than anything else in their whole life and made it twice as hard for them to be happy and succeed at anything, especially their marriages. Finally, suppose X undermined your society as surely as termites undermine a house. Suppose X turned the bricks your society was made of into sand. It destroyed the most fundamental of all building blocks of society, the family. Suppose X did to millions what it did to your family: it destroyed people; it destroyed lives; it destroyed your society. Now imagine X didn't have anything to do with sex. Wouldn't X be universally condemned? Would any sane human being speak up in defense of X? Would anybody even tolerate X? Yet those three things are exactly what divorce does, and yet you tolerate it; you defend it; you do it. Yes, I know you'll come back with your media lies about how divorce doesn't really do that, just as you give us lies about postabortion trauma being a myth.

Libby: Oh, we're *liars* now, are we?

'Isa: Yes, you're liars. If you're baby killers, why shouldn't you be liars? Why should we expect murderers to be honest? If you're willing to kill your kids, why should we trust you not to kill the truth?

Libby: [Expletive—and other words—deleted.] Professor, this is simply outrageous. I am appalled at your words . . .

'Isa: But you're not appalled at the facts! Just at the words that tell the truth about them.

Libby: I'm appalled at your betrayal of your promise to be logical.

'Isa: I'm being logical!

Libby: You're appealing to passion.

'Isa: I'm appealing to the law of noncontradiction, to logical consistency. Betrayal is universally condemned, betraying people, breaking solemn promises—unless it's sexual. Justice and honesty and not doing other people harm, all these moral demands are accepted—until they interfere with sex. Helping society, building it up, improving others' lives—everyone admires this, until it involves sex. Now who's being logically consistent, and who's not?

Libby: So America is going to hell because we're having too much sex.

'Isa: That's not what I said. It's not the quantity; it's the quality. You can't have "too much sex" if it's in the right place, and the right place is marriage. That's what it's *for*.

Libby: Says who? Says you and your religion. But not mine.

'**Isa:** No, not just my religion; my body. And yours too. How could you miss such an obvious point? That's what it's *for*—how can that simple point be so threatening that you put your moral eyes out to avoid seeing it?

Libby: Oh, I guess it's because I'm a part of the Great Satan, America on the road to hell.

'**Isa:** I didn't say America was going to hell either. In fact, I'm impressed that most of the rest of traditional morality is still popular, and believed, and taught, even on TV. Your sitcoms and your soap operas, and your movies—they never glorify murder or rape or stealing, or even lying. But they always glorify fornication, and adultery, and sodomy, and abortion, and contraception. They tell you to control your drug addictions and your alcohol addictions and your violence addictions and your gun addictions and even your smoking addictions and your overeating addictions, everything except your sex addictions.

Libby: You know what you are? You are the religious right personified.

'**Isa:** Because I'm against abortion and sodomy and adultery and divorce and fornication and contraception and condoms?

Libby: Yes.

'**Isa:** Do you know what you just said? Do you know who you just found out? Whose real identity you just discovered? Your definition of the religious right—that's me, not you, right?—that's the practical difference between us, our nonnegotiable difference, right?

Libby: Yep.

'**Isa:** Well, you just gave my side a great hero, and you just lost one. Because you just defined Doctor Martin Luther King.

[The dialogue resumes after an interruption that we all agreed not to include.]

Libby: Can you finish your sermon quickly, Professor? Again I'm running short on tape and on patience. I think it would be helpful if you could connect your—your last remarks (I was going to say "your diarrhetic diatribe". See how polite I can be?)—connect your remarks on sex with the whole point of these interviews, moral absolutism.

'**Isa:** The connection is that the driving force of moral relativism in your society seems to be almost exclusively sexual.

Libby: What exactly do you mean by that?

'**Isa:** I mean exactly this: you use the philosophy of relativism to justify knocking each other up whenever you feel like it.

Libby: [Sigh.] We need to finish our job here. So perhaps you could answer just two more questions. If sexual addiction is the cause of moral relativism, what is the cause of sexual addiction, and what is its cure? Perhaps you would like to end on those two questions.

'**Isa:** In two minutes or less?

Libby: Yes, please.

'**Isa:** All right, here's my guess at the cause. I think once you've lost God, once you've become a secularist, you have only two substitutes, only two experiences that can still give you the mystical thrill that God gives, that God designed all souls to get, and to demand until they get it. They are sex and death.

Libby: You call death a "thrill"? Like sex?

'**Isa:** Yes. Both sex and death are thrills because they're ecstasies, in the literal sense of the word: standing-outside-yourself, out-of-body experiences. But you've secularized death into just another "learning experience", or just another stage of life to accept blandly and limply, like a nice night's sleep. So the only God-like thing left is sex.

Libby: Unless you surf.

'**Isa:** Yes! You *do* understand some things. But that doesn't do any harm. That's innocent.

Libby: What about drugs?

'**Isa:** I think they have the same appeal. I've never done them—not even alcohol—but I think they feed the same need; they promise the same mystical thrill: the transcending of reason and self-consciousness and personal moral responsibility. They just don't have the . . . the ontological greatness of sex. God invented sex, we invented drugs, so sex has to have much more in it. It has a depth, like the sea. And a mystery, a great mystery.

Libby: But you say the sex addict is looking for the same thing as the drug addict?

'Isa: Yes. He's looking for God.

Libby: Somehow I thought you'd say that. Seriously, do you really think he's also looking for *morality*?

'Isa: Oh, no. He's looking to transcend morality.

Libby: So that's why he's a fool?

'Isa: No, maybe that's why he's a natural mystic. You know, I really believe the addict—the sex addict or the drug addict—is closer to the deepest truth than the mere moralist. Does that shock you? Yes, I thought it would. I think the addict is looking for the very best thing in some of the very worst places. He's looking for heaven; he's looking for a transcendence of self-consciousness and moral responsibility; he's looking for the state of mind that the saints in heaven have and that mystics have for brief moments on earth.

Libby: Unconsciously, you mean.

'Isa: Yes.

Libby: So he's right.

'Isa: He's wrong to demand it *now*, and he's wrong to refuse the other state of consciousness, the normal state, and he's wrong to try to get it through drugs or through illicit sex or through alcohol or through anything else that God forbids. But he's not wrong to want it. Because God designed us all for it—for that mystical state where morality is transcended or transformed, that mystical marriage that the mystics speak of.

Libby: Good grief, Professor, you're a real surprise today. You're much sexier than Muslims are supposed to be!

'Isa: I know most of my fellow Muslims will say I'm a heretic for this, but I think the Sufis are right there. I'm not a Sufi, and I think their theology is blasphemous, but I think they're onto something with this mystical marriage. Your Jewish and Christian mystics say the same thing. Mount Sinai was not the Promised Land, after all; Mount Zion was. And Mount Sinai isn't Mecca either. But it's an indispensable step on the way there. Morality is the road to mysticism. Submission is the way to ecstasy.

Libby: And earthly sex is a distraction?

'Isa: No, I think earthly sex is a tiny foretaste of the mystical union; you might want to call it a sacrament, a sacred sign. Almost all the mystics use sexual imagery.

Libby: Most Muslims don't, though; isn't that right? You don't speak about *loving* Allah, unless you're Sufis.

'Isa: That's right. We don't cozy up to God. And neither do your Christian saints. When the real God appears in your Scriptures, they "fall at his feet as though dead". But we love God's character; we love what God is: goodness, righteousness, holiness, perfection, charity, unselfishness. That's why we're moral absolutists.

Libby: But you just said morality isn't ultimate after all, just a stage on the way to mysticism.

'Isa: It's not *ultimate*, but it *is* absolute. It's not the last thing, but it's the first thing, the necessary thing, the necessary way to the last thing.

Libby: You mean if we're good, we'll go to heaven and have mystical experiences.

'Isa: Yes. Now you're speaking simply and clearly. Like my namesake (blessed be his name): "Blessed are the pure of heart, for they shall see God."

Libby: And now, finally, what would you suggest as the cure for moral relativism? We haven't gotten to our last question yet, and we have only a minute left. If the world is as bad off as you say, what can save it? Good philosophy?

'Isa: No, this disease needs a stronger medicine. We need good philosophy, because bad philosophy is justifying bad living, but we need something else much more.

Libby: What?

'Isa: We need saints. No, we need to *be* saints. Only saints can save the world.

Libby: And there we have it, folks. I guess that about wraps it up. "Only saints can save the world"—the cure for moral relativism according to Professor 'Isa Ben Adam. This is Liberty Rawls reporting from Martha's Vineyard, where the sun is bright and the surf is up.

'Isa: I like my ending better.

Afterword

For those who may be interested in learning more about the two people in this book, 'Isa and Libby—and also Alexander Solzhenitsyn, the ghost of Thorwald Erikson (Leif Erikson's son), three popes, the sea serpent, Aristotle, Bucky Dent, the heroes of the Great Blizzard of '78 and the Palestinian *intifadah*, the Norns, the victims of postabortion trauma, armless nature mystics, Cortez, Montezuma, Quetzalcoatl, the girl in Matthew 24:41, deaf and blind Caribbean dancers, Mary Monthly, Jewish mother substitutes, the god Ulmo, Dutch Calvinists, the Wandering Jew, the demon Hurricano, and the Islam of body surfing—the story of how they all came together in 1978 will be told in the forthcoming *Sea Full of Angels*.